SAILING MADE SIMPLE

SAILING MADE SIMPLE

Shirley H.M. Reekie

Champaign, Illinois

Library of Congress Cataloging-in-Publication Data

Reekie, Shirley H.M., 1953-
    Sailing made simple

    Bibliography: p.
    Includes index.
    1. Sailing.   2. Sailing—Study and teaching
I. Title.
GV811.R364   1987   797.1'24   86-10393
ISBN 0-88011-278-6

Developmental Editor: Steve Houseworth
Copy Editor: Olga Murphy
Production Director: Ernie Noa
Typesetter: Theresa Bear
Text Design: Julie Szamocki
Text Layout: Lezli Harris
Illustrations by: Jerry A. Korb: California Design Drafting Services
Cover Design: Jack Davis
Cover Photo: Berg & Associates/Kirk Schlea
Printed By: Versa Press

ISBN 0-88011-278-6

Printed in the United States of America

10 9 8 7 6 5 4 3 2 1

Leisure Press
A division of Human Kinetics Publishers, Inc.
Box 5076, Champaign, IL 61820

Dedication

For my father,
who taught me to sail
in the ''Towards you, away from you'' style
and for my mother,
who always had a meal ready when I came in.

Thank you to both of you.

Contents

Preface

One problem in learning to sail is that before you attempt to go out sailing for the first time you must know and understand many principles of safe sailing. You can't simply read chapter 1 of this book and then immediately go out sailing expecting to use only those skills. How do you get the sails up, launch the boat, sail with or against the wind, dock the boat, and return safely? If all that were covered in chapter 1, the chapter would be immensely long, meaningless, and confusing, making you hesitant and the rest of the book extremely short.

Each chapter begins with an outline of the skills and knowledge to be mastered and a list of all the new terms introduced in that chapter. Each new term is printed in italic type the first time it is used. A glossary of sailing terms is also provided at the end of the book. At the end of each chapter are questions and activities to test your understanding, with the answers provided in Appendix D. At the end of each part of the book is a self-graded quiz to help you review the material covered in each part.

This book is divided into three parts. Carefully read and understand part 1 *before* going on the water, unless you are fortunate enough to have an experienced sailor on board guiding you along. Undoubtedly, you'll want to get out on the water as soon as possible, but you must study this section first. The ideal situation would include a swimming ability test and a capsize drill on the first day so that you at least have had contact with the boat and the water.

In each chapter of part 2 the basic practical sailing skills are presented in order of need.

Read the chapter first; then try the procedures on land, where appropriate, and then on the water. Afterwards, review every aspect and answer any lingering questions. Through this step-by-step process, you will learn to sail easily without being overwhelmed with terms, techniques, and procedures.

In part 3 you will learn the basics of the three branches of sailing—racing, boardsailing, and cruising. You may wish to try them after completing parts 1 and 2. Small boat sailing forms a good foundation for each of these areas.

British terminology, where it differs from U.S. usage, is included in square brackets and is shown as follows: vang [kicking strap].

Acknowledgments

Thanks to those who read my first attempts at writing this book, particularly to my brother, Andrew, who also drafted most of the illustrations. Thanks to all those who asked me questions at Trearddur Bay Sailing Club, The Ohio State University, and San Jose State University, thus helping me to understand further. Finally, thanks to all those who have crewed for me and whose initials are painted on my boat, including Ellen, John, Susan, David, and Megan, but particularly Peter.

Part 1
Preparing To Sail

1

Evolution and Function of Sailboats

Learning to sail is not really difficult. Like all other technical activities, however, sailing must be learned in progressive stages. For the novice, the first stage is to understand the evolution and function of sailboats.

Objectives

- To understand basic sailing terminology
- To know how sailboat design developed
- To give a boat's sail setting for any course
- To answer the questions on p. 8

Helpful Terms

Mast. Vertical pole up which sail is hoisted.

Hull. Floating part of the boat, the body.

Rig. Configuration of mast(s) and sail(s).

Running. Sailing in the same direction that the wind is blowing.

Reaching. Sailing across the wind, at 90° to its direction.

Centerboard/daggerboard. Vertical fin protruding under boat.

Wind direction. Direction *from* which wind blows.

Luffing. Heading the front of the boat into the wind so the sail flutters and the boat slows.

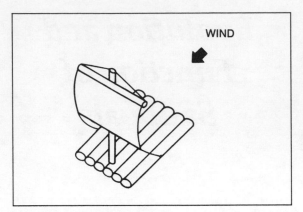

Figure 1-1   Simple sailboat

Tacks.   Zigzag courses perpendicular to each other by which a boat may progress toward the wind.

Beating/sailing close-hauled.   Sailing at 45° to the direction from which the wind is coming.

What Sailing Offers You

Few sports offer the range of possibilities that sailing offers. You may have been attracted to the sport by watching boats on one of those cloudless days and thought how peaceful and relaxing sailing looks. It can be. Perhaps you have watched boats take off on a windy day, spraying water out to the sides, and thought how exhilarating it looks. It can be this, too. Maybe you want to try sailing because it is a sport to enjoy at any stage of life from 5 to 85. Sailing can mean the excitement of competitve racing or the relaxation of a solitary outing. Sailing can be for everyone—in many weathers.

Whatever your age or previous lack of sailing experience, this book is for you. Even if you've had a frightening sailing experience that left you fearful, this book will help you conquer that fear. Nothing is assumed, and every new term, maneuver, or principle is italicized and accompanied by an explanation.

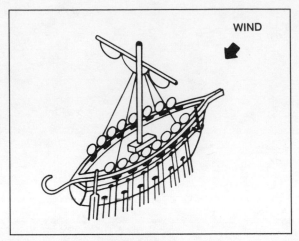

Figure 1-2   Roman trireme

Evolution and Function of Sailboats

Sailboats are built in many styles and sizes designed for specific functions. You may not have thought much about why boats are designed with special features. However, people who depended upon sailboats for food, income, and travel have experimented over thousands of years with boat design to improve each boat's effectiveness. This section will help you understand how boat design affects boat function and how you can better use your boat.

How Sailboats Evolved

Have you ever wondered why a sailboat is designed the way she is? (A boat is always referred to as "she.") Let's look briefly at their development over the years. Perhaps the first sailboat was a log or raft; then someone put up a pole, called a *mast*, that projected upward at a 90° angle to the boat and attached to it a simple sail to catch the wind (see Figure 1-1).

This idea worked fine—as long as the sailors wanted to go in the same direction that the wind blew. But if the wind was against them, the sail would not work and the sailors had

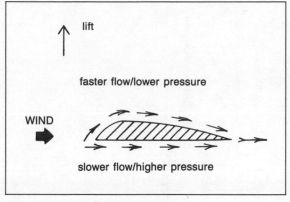

Figure 1-3 Ship of Columbus's time

Figure 1-4 Clipper ship

lift

faster flow/lower pressure

WIND

slower flow/higher pressure

Figure 1-5 Air flow over wing

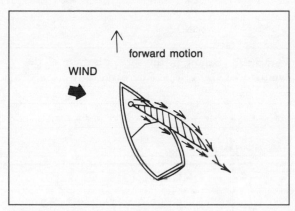

forward motion

WIND

Figure 1-6 Air flow past sail

to paddle or row. For example, Roman triremes used many layers of slave-powered oars to propel the boat against the wind (see Figure 1-2).

By the late 1400s, around the time of Columbus, boat design had been refined (see Figure 1-3) to include some triangular sails.

Finally, sailors were able to adjust the angle of the sails to the wind, and as a result, they could sail both with and across the wind. Because the floating part of the boat, or *hull*, offered resistance to being pushed sideways through the water, the resultant direction of the boat was forward and a little sideways. Hull shape changed over the years from flat to curved and from rotund to sleek, as sailors sought to sail faster and to continue to have boats capable of carrying large loads. As world trade increased, boats needed to be more sea-

worthy to combat the heavy seas. Some square-sailed ships such as the famous clipper ships, which were fast and designed to make use of the prevailing trade winds, remained in use into the last century (see Figure 1-4).

Increasingly, however, the shape and placement of the sails and mast, or the *rigs*, have changed to enable boats to sail much closer to the direction from which the wind is coming and yet still make forward progress. The concern of modern sailboats is not to carry vast loads but to be designed for speed and maneuverability. Here, briefly, is the way a sailboat harnesses the wind.

How Sailboats Work

When a sail is filled with wind, it takes up

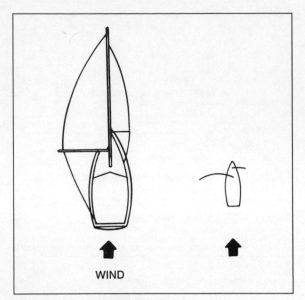

Figure 1-7 Sailing in the same direction as the wind

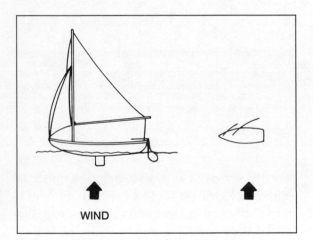

Figure 1-8 Sailing across the wind

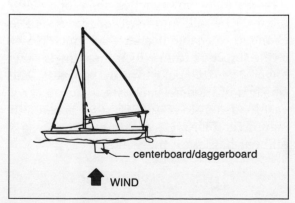

Figure 1-9 Centerboard/daggerboard

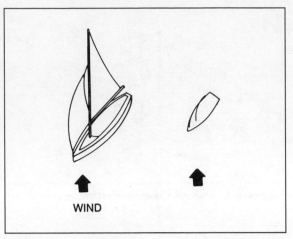

Figure 1-10 Sailing at 45° to the wind

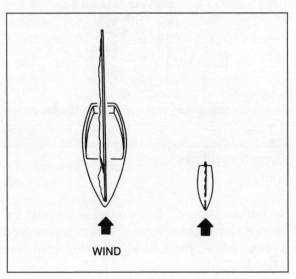

Figure 1-11 Sailing into the wind—luffing

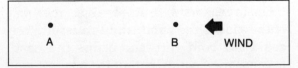

Figure 1-12 Proposed course: from A to B

an airfoil shape like the wing of an airplane (see Figure 1-5).

As air splits to pass the obstruction, some flows in an almost straight line; however, the air flowing past the curved edge has a longer

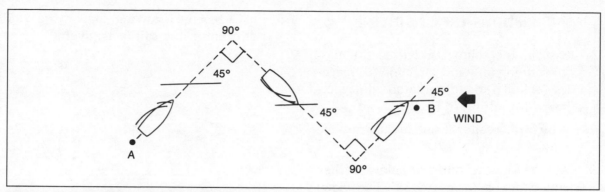

Figure 1-13 Beating/sailing close-hauled from A to B

pathway to travel. For the two flows to rejoin, the air passing by the longer, curved side must travel faster than the airflow on the straight side. This faster-moving airflow causes a decrease in pressure, either above a plane's wing, giving it lift, or in front of a sailboat's sail, giving it forward motion (see Figure 1-6).

When sailing, you can adjust the angle of the sail to the boat, causing the boat to sail at almost any angle to the wind. A modern sailboat uses this sailing principle. Like the early raft, the boat in Figure 1-7 can easily sail in the same direction as the wind.

Notice that she has her sails all the way out; this direction of sailing is called *running*.

With the sail pulled in about halfway, the boat in Figure 1-8 may sail across the wind; this is called *reaching*.

The tendency to be pushed sideways by the wind is reduced by a fin, called a *centerboard* or *daggerboard* (see Figure 1-9), that protrudes down through the hull into the water below the boat.

If the sail is pulled in as far as possible, and the centerboard is pushed all the way down into the water, a boat can still go forward, rather than sideways, when sailing at about 45° to the *wind direction*, or the direction from which the wind is coming (see Figure 1-10).

Some high-performance boats can sail even more closely to the wind, but none can sail

directly into the wind. If you tried to point your boat into the wind, your sails would no longer take up an airfoil shape but would flap about, or *luff*, like a flag, and your boat would be unable to go forward (see Figure 1-11).

If you continued to point into the wind for long enough, you would eventually start to drift backward.

You may be thinking that if a boat cannot sail any closer to the source of the wind than 45°, how could it ever be possible to get from A to B as in Figure 1-12?

You cannot sail there directly, but you can get there by sailing a zigzag course—first 45° to the wind one way, then 45° to the wind the other way. These zigzagging lines in Figure 1-13 are called *tacks*, and your boat is said to be *beating* or sailing *close-hauled* while getting from A to B.

This would be a good time to go outside and observe some boats sailing. You'll probably notice things you hadn't before. For example, notice how far out a boat's sail protrudes. Can you determine from where the wind is coming? Then watch what happens when a boat turns into the wind.

To check for comprehension, answer the following questions. If you answered them correctly, go on to chapter 2, or reread this chapter and ask your instructor or an experienced sailor to explain those things you do not understand. Answers are on p. 131.

Questions on Chapter 1

1. Explain the following terms: (a) mast (b) running (c) wind direction (d) reaching (e) hull (f) rig (g) centerboard/daggerboard (h) luffing (i) beating.

2. Why can't a sailboat sail directly into the wind?

3. Are the sailboats outlined below (as they would appear from a bird's-eye view) running, reaching, or beating? (The arrow is the wind direction.)

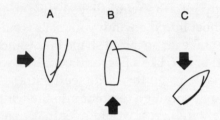

4. In each of the following, draw in the sail if the wind is as given.

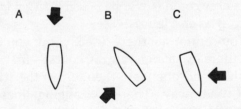

5. In each of the following, draw in the wind direction if the sail is as given.

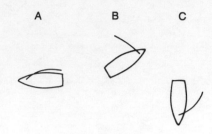

Activities for Chapter 1

1. Observe some boats sailing. Use the position of their sails to identify those that are running, reaching, or beating.

2. Use the sail insignia chart in Appendix B to identify some of the boats you see sailing.

3. When you have identified a boat that is beating, observe her closely for a few minutes to see if she makes progress toward the wind by zigzagging. Use the blank area below to plot the courses of boats you observed.

2

Points of Sailing

Now that you have learned how a sailboat works, you can understand the adjustments to make for sailing in different directions.

Objectives

- To know the names of all the directions a boat may sail
- To understand why a boat's sail setting varies
- To recognize boats on port and starboard tacks
- To answer the questions on p. 14

Helpful Terms

Bow. Front of boat.

Windward. Side over which the wind blows first, the windy side.

Leeward. Side over which the wind blows last, the sheltered side.

Points of sailing. Various directions in which a boat may sail relative to the wind.

Heading. Direction a boat is pointed.

Jib. Small triangular sail in front of the mast.

Wing and wing. Running, with sails out on either side of the boat.

No-go zone. Sector of approximately 45° either side of the wind (90° in total) into which it is impossible to sail.

Tiller. Stick held to control the rudder and to steer the boat.

Rudder. Fin at back of the boat used to turn the boat.

Falling off. Altering course to head more away from the wind (also known as **bearing away**).

Heading up. Altering course to head more toward the wind (also known as **bearing up**).

Pinching. Sailing so close to the wind that the sail begins to luff.

Port. Left side of the boat, looking toward the front.

Starboard. Right side of the boat, looking toward the front.

Determining Wind Direction

The manner in which a boat sails from one place to another is determined by the wind direction in relation to the boat's course; therefore, you must be absolutely certain you know from where the wind is coming the entire time you are sailing. The wind direction is a reference point from which everything else is determined. Some people never clearly establish this reference point and never know exactly where their sails should be set. Always know from where the wind is coming before you start sailing.

The following are a few efficient ways to determine the wind's direction—and two ways not to try!

- Stand and face into the wind, feeling it on your cheeks. When the wind is blowing on both cheeks equally, the wind is coming from ahead of you. Sound can also determine wind direction. Close your eyes and concentrate on hearing the wind equally in each ear. This sensitivity takes time to develop, so start practicing now instead of waiting until your first sail.

- Look around for flags, streamers, or smoke, for they will be blowing in the same direction as the wind. Keep watching for a second or two to average out the small differences.

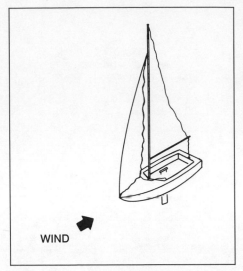

Figure 2-1 A boat headed into the wind

- Look for ripples on the water's surface. Ripples are blown along with the wind with their long edges at 90° to the wind. If you use this method, be careful not to confuse ripples generated by the wind with ripples generated by water currents.

- Observe the way anchored or moored boats float. A boat anchored by the *bow* or front will float so that the bow points into the wind. In tidal waters, check if it is really the wind blowing the boat, rather than the current acting on the hull.

- Watch other boats sailing. When their sails are flapping and over the midline of the boat, the boat is headed into the wind (see Figure 2-1).

With experience, you'll be able to determine the direction of the wind by simply looking at any boat and observing her sail setting.

- Low clouds scudding across the sky can easily indicate the wind direction, but they also warn inexperienced sailors that the sailing conditions are too windy.

- Do *not* use the "wet finger" method, which is imprecise, nor the "tree leaves" method,

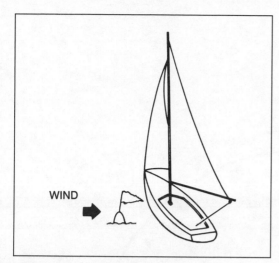

Figure 2-2 Windward/leeward

which works well only in a hurricane, when you would be advised not to sail!

Two other terms relating to wind direction are *windward* and *leeward*, (pronounced ''looard''). The former is the side over which the wind blows first, and the latter is the more sheltered side.

In Figure 2-2 the left side is the windward side of the boat: The buoy is to windward of the boat; the boat is to leeward of the buoy.

Points of Sailing

Now that you realize the importance of knowing the direction of the wind, you can understand how a boat sails on various courses. *Points of sailing* are the various directions a boat may sail in relation to the wind. In chapter 1 you learned the terms *running, reaching,* and *beating.* This chapter explains them in more detail so that you will know how to adjust your sail according to where you are pointing the boat, or *heading,* and in relation to the wind's direction. For every point of sailing, the goal is to harness all the power possible by adjusting the sail to the correct angle in relation to the wind.

Figure 2-3 shows all the points of sailing on which a boat may sail.

Running

Boats 1 and 2 of Figure 2-3 are sailing with the wind, or running. Notice that to do this efficiently, you will have your sail(s) all the way out to catch as much wind as possible. If you have a small triangular sail in front of the mast, called a *jib*, and you are sailing exactly downwind, the jib should be all the way out on the opposite side to the mainsail; otherwise, it would have all the wind stolen from it by the mainsail. This sail position is called *sailing wing and wing* [goosewinging] and is the only point of sailing where the main and jib are on opposite sides (see Figure 2-4).

In running, the centerboard can be pulled up because it is not needed to stop your boat from slipping sideways, but it should be left in the slot ready to be pushed down again. Leaving it down produces unnecessary drag and slows the boat.

Reaching

When sailing across the wind, or reaching (Boats 5 and 6 of Figure 2-3), you must have your sails halfway out. This halfway position is efficient for converting wind coming across the boat into forward sailing. Reaching is generally the fastest point of sailing. Here the sideways push is greater than when running, so the centerboard should be positioned halfway down (see Figure 2-5).

This is a compromise position between having the resistance to sideways slipping that is needed and still keeping the drag to a minimum.

Beating/Sailing Close-Hauled

When trying to sail as closely as possible toward the direction from which the wind is

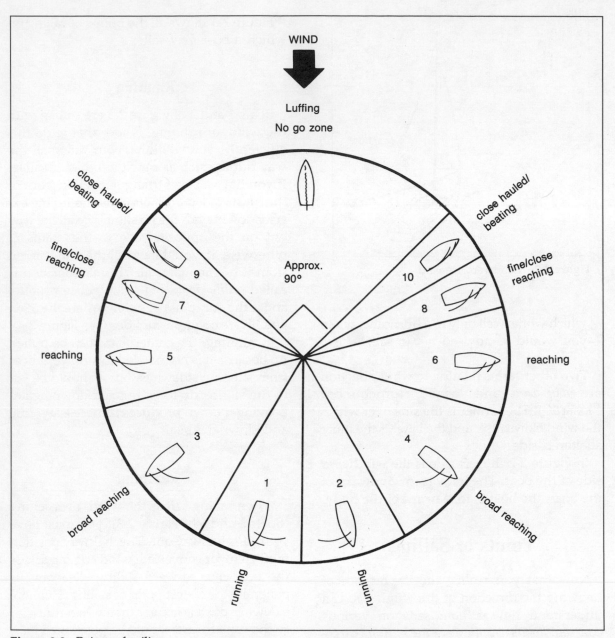

Figure 2-3   Points of sailing

coming, pull in your sails tightly. This position has two different names, both used interchangeably. You are said to be beating or to be sailing close-hauled when in Positions 9 and 10 of Figure 2-3. This close-in position of the sail is the most efficient for sailing as closely as possible to the wind's direction. If you alter course from this heading to sail more

into the wind, the sails will begin to flap, or luff, because the wind is now beginning to blow equally over both sides of the sail; plus, the boat gets no forward drive in such a situation. You have entered the *no-go zone*. Refer back to Figure 2-1 for an illustration.

When you notice your sail luffing, alter course back again to a direction more across

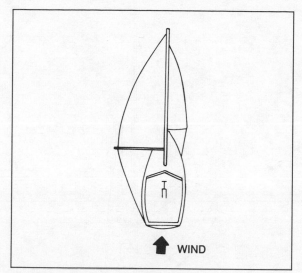

Figure 2-4 Sailing with the wind—running; sailing wing and wing

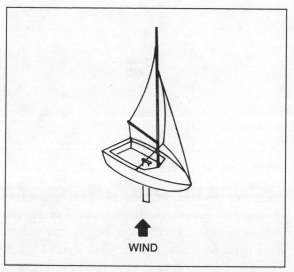

Figure 2-6 Sailing close to the wind—beating/close-hauled

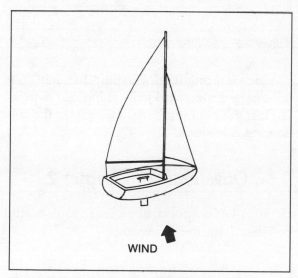

Figure 2-5 Sailing across the wind—reaching

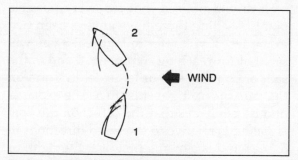

Figure 2-7 Falling off/bearing away

Falling Off and Heading Up

Altering course more away from the wind is called *falling off*, or *bearing away* (see Figure 2-7).

If someone calls out "Fall off," you are probably being asked to alter your course, not to fall off the boat into the water! The opposite, when you head more toward the wind, is called *heading up*, or *bearing up* (see Figure 2-8).

If you head up too far and the sail flaps a little, even when it is pulled in tightly, you are *pinching*—that is, trying to sail closer to the wind than its direction will allow. As a result, you will move slowly as in Figure 2-9.

the wind by pulling the *tiller*, which controls the *rudder*, toward the nonsail side. This will stop the sails luffing and will move you forward again. A great sideways pressure occurs in beating that must be converted into forward motion; consequently, the centerboard must be pushed all the way down into the water to give the maximum resistance possible to sideways slipping (see Figure 2-6).

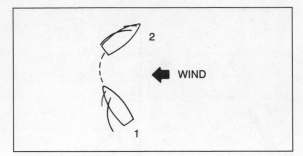

Figure 2-8   Heading/bearing up

Of course, you can also sail in many intermediate directions so that 3 and 4 of Figure 2-3, between a run and a reach, are called broad reaches; and 7 and 8, between a reach and a beat, are termed fine, or close reaches.

Symmetry of Points of Sailing

Have you noticed that for every possible point of sailing there have always been two examples? If you refer to Figure 2-3 you will see that for reaching, Numbers 5 and 6, the sails are on the *port*, or left side, in 5 and on the *starboard*, or right side, in 6. The explanation is, as always that the direction the boat is sailing is relative to the wind direction. In 5, the wind is blowing first over the right, or starboard side, and in 6 the wind blows first over the port, or left side. Thus 5 and 6 can be fully described as being on a starboard reach, or a port reach, respectively. *No!* Those are not in the wrong order! A boat with the wind blowing first over her left, or port side, is on a port reach or port run or port beat. Of course, a boat with the wind blowing first over her right, or starboard side, is on a starboard reach or starboard run or starboard beat. Remember: Whether a boat is said to be on port tack or on starboard tack is determined by which side the wind hits first, not by the side on which the sails are. In other words, if the sails are on the port side, the boat's course is a starboard beat or reach or run.

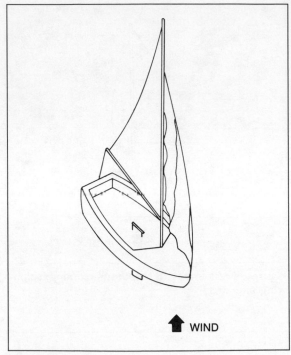

Figure 2-9   Pinching

Much important information that may take longer to understand fully is in this chapter. To test your comprehension, answer the following questions.

Questions on Chapter 2

1.   On which point of sailing (run, reach, beat) are the following?

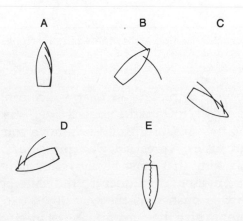

2. On which tack (port or starboard) are the following?

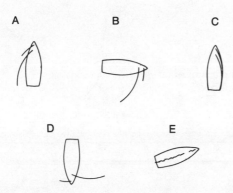

3. What would be the complete description for these boats' headings (e.g., port reach, starboard beat)?

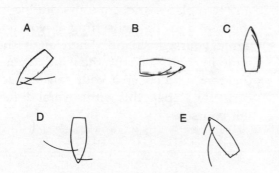

4. Suppose you were to start from Point A and steer for Point B. What would be the most efficient sail setting (e.g., pulled in tight on the right side; let out all the way on the left)?

5. (a) Which is the leeward boat in this diagram?

   (b) How could you describe the position of the buoy relative to the boats?

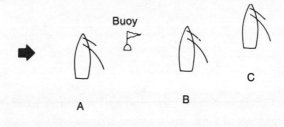

6. Which of these boats has fallen off and which has headed up?

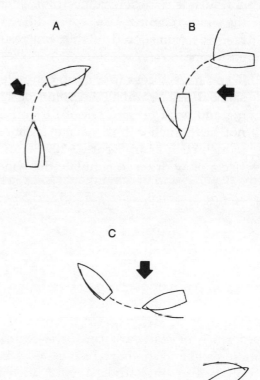

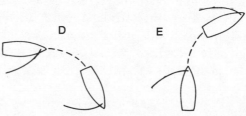

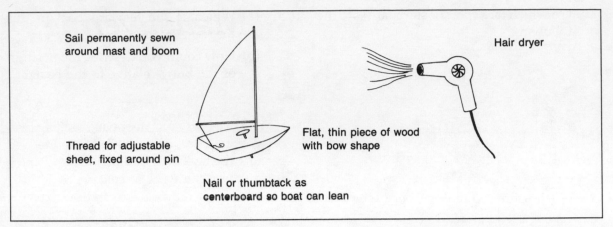

Sail permanently sewn
around mast and boom

Hair dryer

Thread for adjustable
sheet, fixed around pin

Flat, thin piece of wood
with bow shape

Nail or thumbtack as
centerboard so boat can lean

Figure 2-10   Model sailboat and "wind"

Activities for Chapter 2

1. Go outside and determine from where the wind is coming. Use several different methods. You should get the same result each time.

2. If you have access to a radio-controlled sailboat, sail her on all the points of sailing and head up and fall off. If you do not have such a boat, make a simple model, such as in Figure 2-10.
   Use a blow dryer to simulate the wind, and head your boat on the different points of sailing. Be sure to adjust the sails correctly.

3. Draw an outline of the place you intend to sail. Draw in the wind direction. Pick any two places and draw the outline of the boat and the sail setting as you imagine yourself sailing. Then align the wind in Figure 2-3 with the wind in your diagram, and check if your sails are set correctly. Repeat this with several different courses.

3

Maneuvering

To turn a boat onto any point of sailing, you must maneuver her around. Steering and turning the boat are not difficult if you know from where the wind is coming.

Objectives

- To understand how a boat is steered
- To recognize when a boat comes about and when she gybes
- To demonstrate a land drill for coming about and gybing
- To know the commands for coming about and gybing
- To know how to slow and to stop the boat
- To answer the questions on p. 24

Helpful Terms

In irons. Boat is stationary, heading into the wind with sails luffing.

Coming about. Turning the boat by pointing the bow into the wind, sometimes called **tacking.**

Stern. Back of the boat.

Gybing. Turning the boat by heading the stern into the wind.

Weather helm. Tendency of the boat to turn into the wind and luff.

Boom. Pole along lower edge of mainsail.

Sheet. Rope used to control how far in or out a sail is. (Note that a *sheet* is a *rope*!)

Hiking stick. Extension to the tiller.

Helmsperson. Person steering the boat.

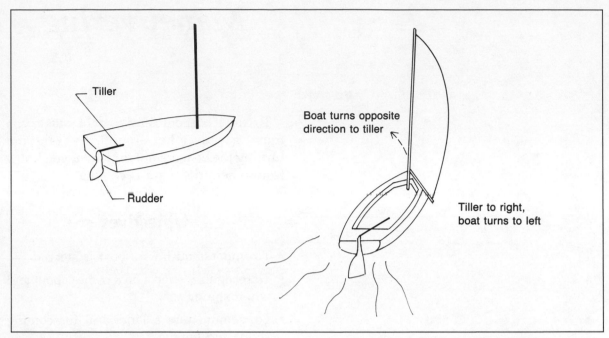

Figure 3-1 Effect of rudder and tiller

Crew. Either all those on board or all except the helmsperson; context specifies meaning.

Quarter. Back corner of the boat between the stern and the side.

Turning the Boat— General Information

Before you set sail, you must master another vital skill—how to steer and turn the boat so that you can return to your starting point! A boat is steered by the tiller, or wheel on large boats, which is connected to a fin, called a rudder, at the back of the boat (see Figure 3-1).

The rudder works by the action of the water flowing past it, so if you move the tiller to the right, the boat will turn to the left, and viceversa. Also, unless the boat is moving through the water, the rudder will have no effect. If you are stationary (*in irons*), the rudder will not work, so use a paddle to turn your boat.

A boat may turn in only two possible directions; and, as you might have guessed, the difference relates to the direction of the wind. To turn your boat around to point the other way, either point her front, or bow, into the wind, which is called *coming* [going] *about* (see Figure 3-2), or by putting her back, or *stern*, into the wind, which is called *gybing*, sometimes spelled *jibing* (see Figure 3-3).

In the initial learning stages of sailing, coming about is safer because it happens more slowly. This type of turn is slow and safe, because during the turn, the boat luffs and has no wind powering her sails. Gybing requires good timing and may occur suddenly and violently if the sailor is unprepared. Wind always powers a gybing boat's sails.

Quickly familiarize yourself with the sensitivity of the tiller on your boat. Experiment by moving it slightly one way then the other, and see what happens to your course. As in a car, when you have turned enough, you must centralize your steering again; otherwise, you will continue to turn. Do not be

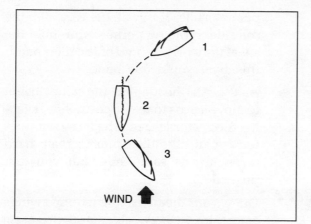

Figure 3-2 Direction of turn—coming about

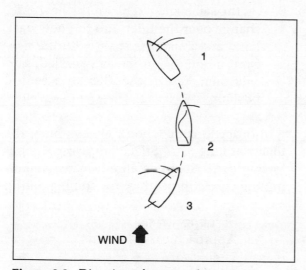

Figure 3-3 Direction of turn—gybing

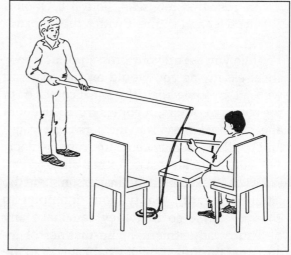

Figure 3-4 Props for your land "boat"

Turning Into the Wind or Coming About

To make a boat come about, sometimes called *tacking*, push the tiller across to the sail side. This will head the boat into the wind and will allow the sails to flap. By keeping the tiller on that side until the sail has filled on the new course, the turn can easily be completed. Practice this maneuver first on land until everything comes naturally. You'll need several "props" to practice coming about on land (see Figure 3-4):

1. A long pole to represent the *boom* (length of metal or wood to which the lower edge of the sail is attached) and someone to move it, as appropriate.

2. Two chairs to represent each side of the boat.

3. A piece of rope to act as the *sheet* (rope that controls how far in or out a sail is).

4. A short pole to act as the tiller and someone to act as a pivot for it at the rudder end. Practice without a *hiking stick* [tiller extention] as you will not be using one

afraid to look behind you to check that the tiller is in the center, but in time, you will know this without looking back. If you let go of the tiller completely and allow the boat to steer herself, she will probably turn into the wind and eventually stop. This heading up tendency is called having *weather helm*. You may, in fact, need to "centralize" the tiller in a position slightly on the side opposite the sail to maintain a straight course.

in your first few sails. Fold it back onto the tiller and secure it with a rubber band.

When you set up your props, position your sheet exactly as you would on the boat you will sail. In some boats the sheet comes from the stern; in others, it comes from the boom ahead of the *helmsperson* (the person steering); and in others, it may come up from the floor.

If you have any *crew* (either all those on board or all except the helmsperson; here the latter is meant), clarify your intention to change course so that they can make any necessary adjustments. The manner of instructing the crew is well-established and the commands are included in the following sequence. This sequence is for turning the boat via heading into the wind, that is, by coming about.

1. As helmsperson, sit on the opposite side to the mainsail. This is almost always the case; only in light winds do you sit on the same side as the sail. Position yourself sitting facing sideways across the boat, steering with the back hand and holding the sheet with the front hand.

2. Get the boat sailing on a close-hauled course. Pull the sail in tightly over the *quarter*, or back corner (see Figure 3-5), and head the boat as close to the wind as possible without the sail flapping.

3. Check around you to make sure you have room to come about. The most important spots to check are the side to which you are turning and behind you; also, check to see if the sheet is free.

4. Alert the crew of your intention to turn the boat by way of heading into the wind by giving the command, ''Ready about.'' Crew responds.

5. Recheck to ensure that no other boats are in your way. If all is clear, say, ''Hard a-lee'' [''Lee-oh''] and, at the same time,

push the tiller firmly all the way onto the sail side. If the rig permits you, hold the sheet under the thumb of the tiller hand; this gives you a free hand.

6. As the boat heads into the wind, begin to move across to the opposite side, keeping the boat balanced. The boat continues to turn and the tiller must remain hard across to the same side that you first pushed it.

7. Duck your head as the boom swings across to the new side, and the crew members take up their new positions opposite the sail again.

8. As the sail begins to fill on the new side, change over the tiller into the new back hand and grasp the sheet with the new front hand. When the sail is filled, and *only* then, return the tiller to a central position.

In order to come about, always push the tiller onto the *SAIL SIDE*. Try using the following (SAILSIDE) as an aid in remembering the correct procedure for coming about:

Sit opposite sail
Approach close-hauled
Is all clear?
Let crew know
Sail side the tiller
Into wind
Duck across
Exchange hands

This takes much practice on the water to perfect. Competent sailors in a good breeze can complete the whole maneuver in a few seconds or less. You must realize that a boat cannot generate any power through the 90° no-go zone referred to in Figure 2-3 so that it is only momentum that carries you around. If you lose this momentum for any reason, you will run out of steam, and the boat will be left stranded with sails luffing, into the

Figure 3-5 Position of sail before coming about

Figure 3-6 Loss of momentum—failing to come about

wind. Use your paddle to complete the turn. The most common way momentum is lost is to start the maneuver from a nonclose-hauled course, and thus you force the boat to use her momentum to turn through more than 90° (see Figure 3-6).

Turning Away From the Wind or Gybing

The opposite maneuver to coming about is gybing (refer back to Figure 3-3), which is turning the stern into the wind. As you will see from the diagrams in Figure 3-7, the major difference between coming about and gybing is that in the former there is a period of time when there is no power in the sails, whereas in gybing there is always power, or wind, in the sails.

Because of the constant wind in the sails, do not attempt gybing in strong winds during your first few sails. If it happens accidently, the worst that can happen is a hard bang on the head from the boom, and/or a wet crew, following a spectacular capsize!

At first, practice on land using the same props as described earlier; then choose a calm day before trying the following on the water:

1. Sit opposite the sail and get the boat sailing on a broad reach. The sail should be almost all the way out without flapping. As always, use the front hand to control the sheet and the back hand to control the tiller.

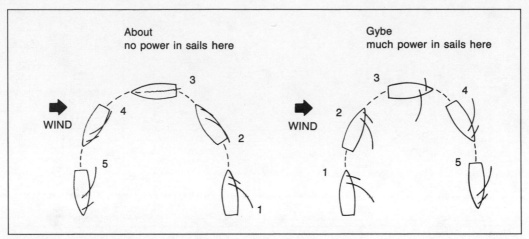

Figure 3-7   Differences of coming about versus gybing

2. Get the boat sailing on a run. Be careful from this point on, because if you turn a few more degrees to the sail side, you will gybe.

3. Check around carefully for boats, especially ''under'' the sail on the side to which you are turning and behind you. Check to make sure the sheet is untangled.

4. Alert the crew of your intention to turn the boat by turning away from the wind with the command, ''Stand by to gybe.'' Crew responds.

5. Recheck for boats on a possible collision course. If all is clear, pull in the mainsheet until the sail is almost all the way in.

6. Helmsperson says ''Gybe-oh'' and, at the same time, pulls the tiller hard across onto the opposite side from the sail. If the rig permits, the grip the sheet by the thumb of the tiller hand, leaving the other hand free.

7. As the boat gybes, the crew members transfer their weight to the new side, keeping low to avoid the swinging boom.

8. At the precise moment the boom reaches its new side (and this happens suddenly),

you *must* return the tiller to the central position. At this same moment, you *must* allow the sheet out to cushion the impact of the boom's swing. Failure to do either may lead to a capsize because the boat leans over too much, and this cannot be corrected easily by the crew's weight.

Remember that in gybing you are pulling the tiller onto the *OPPOSITE* side from the sail. The following (OPPOSITE) may help you remember the order of events in gybing so that they become second nature to you:

On broad reach
Pivot to run
Positions of fleet
Others alerted
Sheet pulled in
Initiate turn
Transfer weight
Ease sheet and center tiller

When you improve your ability you can gybe with the sail full out on the first side; however, be prepared for a violent swing across the boom and have a firm hand to center the tiller.

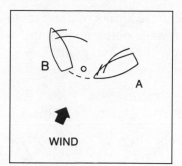

Figure 3-8 Altering course but no about or gybe

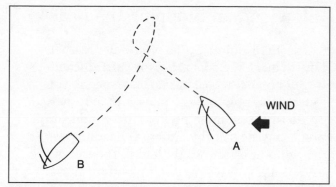

Figure 3-9 Changing tack downwind avoiding the gybe

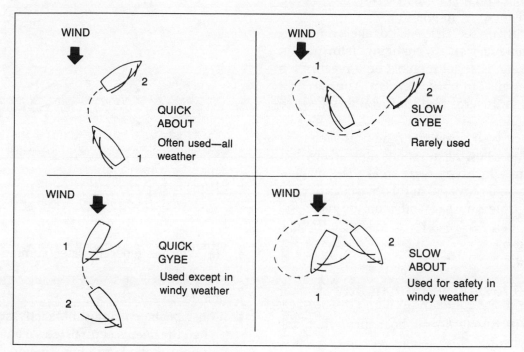

Figure 3-10 Coming about versus gybing

Choosing Which Way to Turn

Altering course does not *have* to include either coming about or gybing. If, for example, you alter course from A to B in Figure 3-8, you merely have to let some sheet out as you move the tiller to change your course from a beat to a broad reach.

The command to the crew would be, "Stand by to fall off to a broad reach."

Another point to remember is that you never *have* to gybe. To get from A to B in Figure 3-9, you could go the long way around and come about, following the sequence explained earlier in this chapter.

This takes more time but it may be safer in windy conditions to avoid gybing.

All of the above means that to change from one course to another you can always choose which way around to go. The fewer degrees you turn through, the more quickly you complete your course change, but you can always turn either way (see Figure 3-10).

Slowing and Stopping the Boat

One final point: So far you have learned how to make the boat move forward efficiently. But because a boat has no brake pedal, you must also know how to slow and stop her. To do this, you must prevent the wind from powering the sails by either (a) heading into the wind and luffing, (b) letting the sail out until it luffs, or (c) combining both of these. All three actions have the same result: a flapping sail and a gradual, but not immediate, loss of forward momentum.

If ever you feel the need to take a time-out, or whenever you are changing helmsperson and crew, first get the boat on a reach, then let the sails out until they flap. You can drift safely in this position until you are ready to sail again.

Check your understanding of this chapter with the following questions. Reread any sections in which you were weak. The maneuvering skills covered in this chapter are used every time you sail and must be mastered completely. Always try to visualize the real situation.

Questions on Chapter 3

1. Which way does a boat turn when she gybes?

2. To which side of the boat do you put the tiller to come about?

3. (a) On which side of the boat should you sit when steering?

    (b) Why?

4. (a) Which way should you face when steering?

    (b) Why?

5. Which of these series of diagrams show boats that have come about, and which show boats that have gybed?

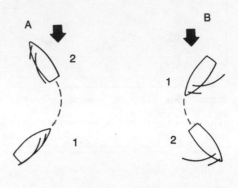

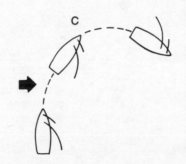

6. (a) Which is generally safer, coming about or gybing?

    (b) Why?

7. Most boats do not sail exactly straight when the tiller is centralized. What is this tendency called, and how do you correct it with the tiller?

Activities for Chapter 3

1. On land, simulate the sequence for coming about.

2. On land, simulate the sequence for gybing.

4

Boat Parts, Knots, and Rigging a Boat

Like all specialized subjects, sailing has its own vocabulary. Now you can review many already familiar terms as well as learn new ones by understanding the function of the parts to which they refer.

Objectives

- To name most boat parts and know their function
- To know how to tie five basic knots
- To rig a boat
- To launch a boat
- To answer the questions on p. 35

Helpful Terms

Gaff. Pole attached to the leading edge of the sail on some rigs to extend the mast upward.

Halyard. Rope used to hoist the sail.

Step. To raise and secure the mast.

Dolly. Wheeled device from which a boat is launched.

Tack. (noun) Lower front corner of a sail; (verb) to turn a boat by heading into the wind.

Shackle. D-shaped link with removable pin.

Jibsnap. Fitting used to attach the leading edge of the jib to the forestay.

Head. Top corner of a triangular sail.

Luff. (noun) Leading edge of a sail; (verb) to flutter.

Fairlead. Eye through which rope is led.

Shroud. Wire holding up the mast.

Bolt rope. Rope sometimes sewn into the luff and/or foot.

Foot. Lower edge of a sail attached to the boom.

Gooseneck. Fitting joining boom with the mast.

Batten pocket. Pocket sewn into a sail to hold the batten.

Batten. Thin strip inserted into a sail

Vang. Rope or wire attached to the boom to hold it down.

Block. Pulley.

Boat Parts

Names for various parts of the boat, introduced in earlier chapters, should now be familiar to you. Quickly check through the Helpful Terms sections of chapters 1, 2, and 3 to make sure you remember them. Learning to sail is a little like learning a new language: It can't be learned overnight.

The following diagrams (Figures 4-1, 4-2, 4-3) cover only the most important boat parts. Because there are so many different types of boats and rigs, select and learn from the diagram that most closely resembles the boat you will sail. An explanation of each term follows. The list may seem long, but when you understand the function of each part, the names will be easier to learn; besides, you already know many of the terms!

Batten. Thin wooden or plastic strip inserted into a pocket in the leech of the sail to make the sail a more efficient shape.

Batten pocket. Pocket sewn into the sail to hold a batten.

Block. Pulley through which a rope is passed to gain a mechanical advantage.

Boltrope. Rope sewn into the luff and foot of the sail giving the edge more strength; in some rigs, often fed along a groove in the mast and/or boom.

Boom. Long, thin piece of wood or metal to which the foot of the sail is attached.

Bow. Front of the boat.

Centerboard/daggerboard. Movable fin whose function is to reduce sideways drift, which protrudes down through the center of the boat.

Cleat. Device of wood, metal, or plastic to which a rope is secured.

Clew. Lower, back corner of a triangular sail.

Downhaul. Rope used to tighten the luff and give the sail a better shape.

Fairlead (pronounced "fairleed"). Eye through which a rope is led.

Foot. Lower edge of the sail.

Forestay. Front shroud attached between the upper part of the mast and the bow to hold up the mast.

Gaff. Long, thin piece of wood or metal attached along the leading edge of the sail above the mast to make an extension to the mast.

Gooseneck. Hinged or swivel fitting that attaches the boom to the mast.

Gudgeon. Fitting that attaches the rudder onto the boat; a pintle fits into it.

Gunwale (pronounced "gunnel"). Top of the side of the boat.

Halyard. Rope used to hoist a sail.

Head. Upper corner of triangular sail. Also, a boat's toilet.

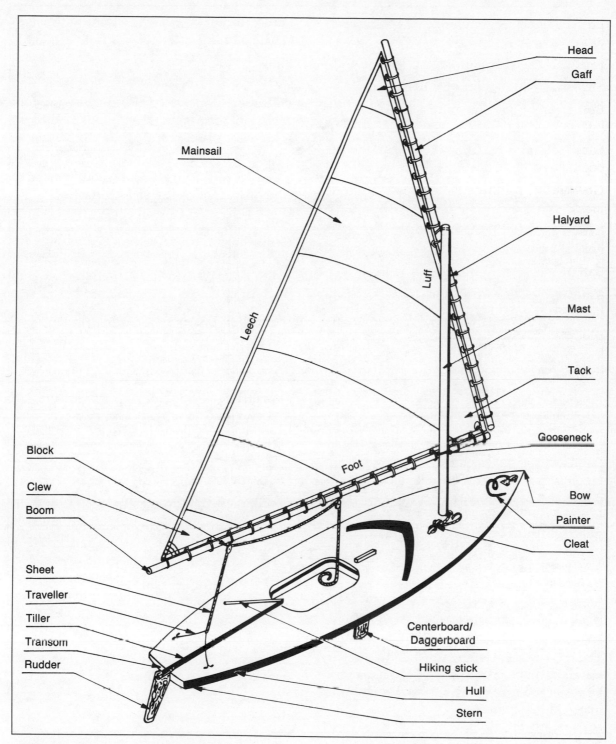

Figure 4-1 Parts of a boat—lateen rig

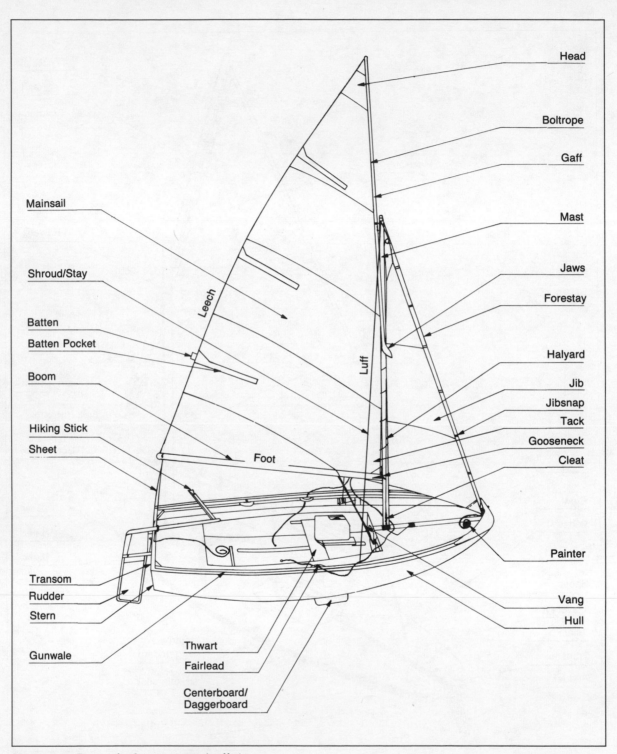

Figure 4-2 Parts of a boat—gunter/gaff rig

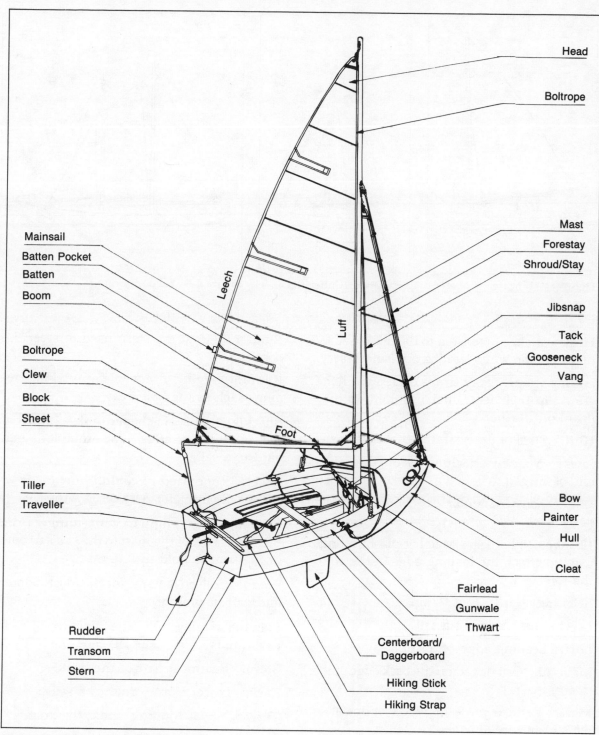

Head

Boltrope

Mainsail

Batten Pocket

Batten

Boom

Mast
Forestay
Shroud/Stay

Jibsnap

Tack
Gooseneck
Vang

Boltrope

Clew

Block

Sheet

Leech

Luff

Foot

Tiller

Traveller

Bow
Painter
Hull

Cleat

Fairlead
Gunwale
Thwart

Rudder

Transom

Stern

Centerboard/
Daggerboard

Hiking Stick

Hiking Strap

Figure 4-3 Parts of a boat—sloop rig

Figure 4-4　Cat rig

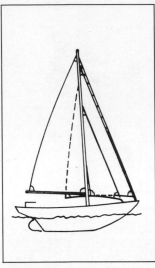

Figure 4-5　Cutter rig

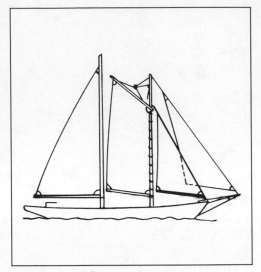

Figure 4-6　Schooner rig

Hiking stick.　Extension to the tiller used by helmsperson when leaning out is necessary.

Hiking straps.　Foot straps under which the crew slip their feet, enabling them to hike [lean] out further.

Hull.　Shell of the boat, the part that floats.

Jaws.　Wooden attachments on the lower end of the gaff to hold it in place on the mast.

Jib.　Small, triangular sail forward of the mast.

Jibsnaps [Jibhanks].　Metal or plastic fittings used to attach the leading edge of the jib to the forestay.

[Kicking strap].　See **Vang.**

Leech.　Back edge of a sail.

Luff.　Leading edge of a sail.

Mainsail.　Sail rigged on the back edge of the (main) mast.

Mast.　Vertical piece of wood or metal to which sails are attached.

Painter.　Piece of rope used to attach the bow to the dock or to tow the boat.

Pintle.　Pin used to attach the rudder to the boat.

Rudder.　Fin at the stern used to steer the boat.

Running rigging.　Movable or working rigging, such as the halyards.

Shackle.　Small, D-shaped link with a pin that unscrews to attach, for example, a halyard to a sail.

Sheet.　Rope used to control how far in or out a sail is. (Note: A sheet is a rope.)

Shroud/stay.　Length of wire running from the upper part of the mast to the sides or bow of the boat to hold up the mast.

Spars.　Collective name for the mast, boom, and gaff (if present).

Standing rigging.　Rigging that is fixed, such as shrouds.

Stern.　Rearmost part of the boat.

Tack.　Lower front corner of a sail.

Thwart.　Seat running across the boat.

Tiller.　Stick attached to the rudder held by the helmsperson when steering the boat.

[Tiller extension.]　See **Hiking stick.**

[Toestraps].　See **Hiking straps.**

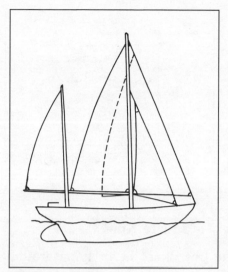

Figure 4-7 Ketch rig

Figure 4-8 Yawl rig

Transom. Extreme back of the boat, the flat vertical part.

Traveller. Track, usually near the stern, to which the mainsheet is attached.

Vang. Rope or wire attached to the boom to hold it down.

Refer to the glossary for additional terms.

Many other types of rigs or sail arrangements exist. Some common boat rigs are illustrated in Figures 4-4, 4-5, 4-6, 4-7, and 4-8.

General Areas of the Boat

Various general areas of a boat and the areas of water in proximity to a boat are shown in Figure 4-9. These general areas apply to all boats, and terms are always applied in reference to the way the boat is pointing. The port side is therefore the left side when looking forward.

Abeam. Perpendicular to the boat.

Aft. At or toward the stern.

Ahead. In front of the boat.

Amidships. Sometimes "midships," toward the center.

Astern. Behind the boat.

Forward. ("for-rad"). Toward the front.

Port. Left side of the boat when looking toward the front.

Starboard. Right side of the boat when looking toward the front.

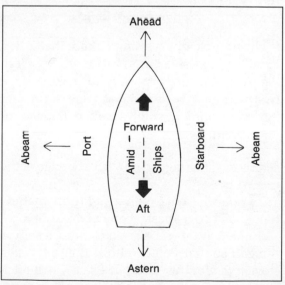

Figure 4-9 General sections of a boat and water nearby

Figure 4-10 Figure eight knot

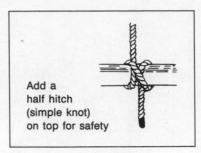

Figure 4-11 Clove hitch

Figure 4-12 Square knot

Knots

Of the many different types of knots, only five basic ones are needed to sail most boats. Without a solid knowledge of these few knots, your boat might float away after you *thought* you had secured her, or your sail might fall down because you *thought* you had secured it. Knots, quite literally, hold a boat together. If you have an instructor, he or she will help you rig your boat the first few times and will check that you have tied the knots correctly. If you are on your own, pay close attention to detail, and test the knot with a sharp tug. Several other knots are shown in chapter 10.

Figure Eight Knot

The figure eight is a simple knot that is tied at the end of a sheet as a "stopper" knot (see Figure 4-10). Its purpose is to make a large obstruction at the end of the rope to prevent it from running through a pulley, fairlead, or your hand.

Clove Hitch

If you sail a boat with a *gaff* (pole that extends sail above mast), you need a knot to attach the *halyard* (rope used to hoist a sail) to the gaff so that you can hoist the sail. Use a clove hitch for this, and put a safety half hitch on top because a clove hitch only holds well when under constant strain (see Figure 4-11).

Square Knot

A square [reef] knot is for tying around something (e.g., a sail when it is down) (see Figure 4-12). A square knot is good for joining together two ropes of equal diameter.

Bowline Knot

The bowline ("bo-lin") is one of the most useful knots. It is used to make a loop that will not slip and become a smaller loop (see Figure 4-13). You might use it to tie up around a post or even to throw to someone as a lifeline. Always check to see if you have tied it correctly by trying to make it slip.

Cleat Hitch

You must be able to secure a rope around a cleat. This is a way of fixing a rope, such as a halyard, so that it is secure yet can quickly be undone (see Figure 4-14). Cleat hitches are good for securing mooring lines to cleats on the dock.

(As you may have noticed, true "knots" use only a rope(s), whereas "hitches" secure a rope around a solid object.)

Rigging the Boat

Rigging the boat means getting her ready to sail. This process will certainly include putting on the sail and hoisting it and will prob-

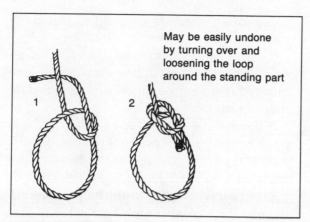

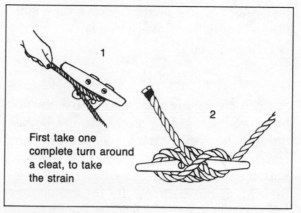

May be easily undone by turning over and loosening the loop around the standing part

Figure 4-13 Bowline knot

First take one complete turn around a cleat, to take the strain

Figure 4-14 Cleat hitch

ably include fitting on the rudder and tiller. If you have car-topped or trailered your boat, you will also have to *step* (raise and secure) the mast. Check to make absolutely certain there are no overhead power cables either near your mast or between your boat and the water. The rigging process varies according to the type of boat, but follow whatever has to be done in this order. If your boat has a jib and you are sailing alone, sail without it at first to keep things simpler.

Assemble Gear

First assemble together everything you, your crew, and your boat will need to sail. This includes life jackets, a paddle, a bailer, the sail(s), the rudder, the tiller, the daggerboard, the halyard, the sheet, and a sponge. Many sailors never set sail without also having a knife, a screwdriver, extra shackles, and short lengths of cord "just in case."

Boat Ashore

If your boat is kept ashore, she should be rigged on shore. Rigging is easier on land because the boat is not moving around, and if you forget something, it is simpler to rectify. A boat on land should be loaded onto a wheeled device for launching called a *dolly*

[trolley]. The bow must be at the same end as the dolly's handle to make for easy launching. Once loaded, the bow of *the boat must be pointed into the wind* so that the sails luff when they are hoisted. On land, the jib should be hoisted first, so you can check the wind direction. Most boats do not sail very well while still on their dollies on land, but they will try! Several methods for finding the wind direction are explained in chapter 2. Turning your head until you hear the wind equally in both ears and feel it equally on both cheeks is one of the simplest. You are now facing into the wind and should point the bow of your boat this way.

If the water near the launch area is congested, first hoist the sails ashore to check them, then lower them before launching the boat. Paddle out to a less congested area, head the boat into the wind, and rehoist the sails.

Boat Afloat

If you are rigging a boat afloat, you must be sure *the bow is pointing into the wind* before putting up the sails. If the boat is moored at the bow and is free to swing, the bow will automatically be pointing into the wind. To keep her lying that way, hoist the mainsail before the jib. You do not want the boat to start sailing before you have finished rigging her—

that would be like switching on a car's ignition with the car already in gear.

Hoist the Jib

If you are sailing with a crew, use the jib, but if you are sailing alone, do not bother hoisting it at all. Attach the bottom front corner of the jib, called the *tack*, to the bow with a small D-shaped link called a *shackle*. Starting at the bottom, clip on the *jibsnaps* [jibhanks] to attach the front of the jib to the forestay. Take care not to twist the sail. Secure the thin, pointed top corner of the jib, called the *head*, to the jib halyard rope with another shackle, or a bowline knot; then slowly raise the sail by pulling on the halyard. Look aloft to see what is happening and never force a sail up if it jams. Find out why. Tighten the halyard until the leading edge of the jib, the *luff*, is taut and wrinkle-free, and cleat the halyard on the port side of the mast. Be sure to coil the excess rope neatly out of the way.

Thread both jib sheet ropes through their *fairleads* (eyes through which ropes are led), either inside or outside the wires (*shrouds*) supporting the mast, depending on which is the straighter pathway. A jib has two sheets because each time you turn, the jib moves across in front of the mast and must be controlled from either side. Tie a figure eight knot at the end of each jib sheet so that they cannot accidentally become unthreaded from the fairlead.

Hoist the Mainsail

The sail must be attached to the boom either by tying at both ends or by feeding a *bolt rope* sewn into the *foot* of the sail into a groove in the boom. In some boats, usually gaff rigged, the sail may be semipermanently attached to the boom. A few boats simply have a mast sleeve into which the mast is inserted before it is stepped. Fix the boom to the mast by means of a hinged or swivel fitting called the *gooseneck*.

If your mainsail has *batten pockets* in the sail into which thin strips of fiberglass (*battens*) are inserted to give the sail a better shape, slide them in, thinner end first.

If the sail has a bolt rope in the luff, this must be fed up a groove in the mast, or gaff. Attach the main halyard to the head of the mainsail with a shackle or a bowline knot; or if it is a boat with a gaff, tie the halyard around the middle of the gaff with a clove hitch. Pull on the halyard to hoist the mainsail, again looking up. Cleat the halyard on the starboard side of the mast when the luff is taut and coil the excess rope neatly.

You may notice some form of rope or wire, called a *vang* [kicking strap], designed to hold the boom down. Usually it runs from a point under the boom near the mast to the foot of the mast; it should always be rigged to ensure that the sail maintains a good shape.

Thread the mainsheet through the pulleys, or *blocks*, and tie a figure eight knot at the end of it, being careful to avoid the swinging boom. The boom should be left to swing free so that the sail does not fill with wind and tip the boat over.

Ready the Rudder, Tiller, and Centerboard

If you have a rudder that pivots up from the water, attach it now, making sure it will not hit the ground. Fit the tiller and check that the mainsheet is not fouled by it. The daggerboard should be readied beside the slot for insertion once you are in deep enough water; or if you have a pivoting centerboard, make sure it is free to go down.

Check Equipment

Check to ensure that life jackets are on and properly adjusted and that paddles/oars and scoops/bailers are on board and tied in.

Launch Stern First

Launch the boat stern first, allowing the sail to run out freely as you turn the boat. When the wind is blowing from the water to the land and you try to launch stern first, the sail will fill with wind, as if on a run. If the wind is strong and the boat seems likely to be tipped off the dolly, do not hoist the sail until after launching and securing the boat head to wind. If possible, always launch the boat to leeward of any obstruction such as a dock or rocks so that your boat will not be blown against it. Hold the boat's bow into the wind while your crew parks the dolly out of the way on land above the high-tide mark, if on the ocean.

Several new terms were introduced in this chapter. You will probably take a while to remember them all, but try the following questions to see how you are doing.

Questions on Chapter 4

1. For what are the following used? (a) rudder (b) sheet (c) halyard (d) stay (e) batten (f) tiller

2. Explain the following: (a) block (b) boltrope (c) boom (d) bow (e) gooseneck (f) port (g) starboard (h) traveller (i) stern

3. (a) In which direction should a boat point when you rig her?

   (b) Why?

4. (a) Ideally, on which side of an obstacle should a boat be launched?

   (b) Why?

Activities for Chapter 4

1. Turn to the list of boat parts on p. 26. For every part listed, find the actual location of that part on the boat you will be sailing.

2. Draw a hull outline on a piece of paper or blackboard. Have everyone in your group either draw in a new part or name one already drawn.

3. Which knot would you use to

   (a) make a loop that will not slip?

   (b) make a stopper knot on the end of a sheet?

   (c) attach the halyard to the gaff?

   (d) make fast a halyard to a cleat?

4. Tie each of the above.

5

Safety Precautions and Capsize Drill

Serious accidents are most unusual in small boat sailing, but they can happen. Before you go for your first sail, you must understand why you should take certain safety precautions and know what to do in case of emergency.

Objectives

- To understand additional basic terminology
- To explain what safety precautions must always be taken
- To know how to avoid capsizing
- To know what to do in the event of a capsize
- To know when and how to give artificial resuscitation
- To recognize the diver's flag
- To answer the questions on p. 43

Helpful Terms

Life jacket/buoyancy aid/personal flotation device (PFD). Jacket worn to aid in floating and survival.

Painter. Rope attached to the front of the boat used for mooring or towing.

Capsize. When a boat tips over.

Bailing. Removing water from the boat.

Preparation for Prevention

Follow the safety precautions described in this chapter, no matter how good a sailor or swimmer you are and no matter how calm the water is.

Most times when people wear car seat belts they are not called upon to save the wearers; rather they are worn for that unexpected occasion that you assume will never happen to you. A sailor wears a *life jacket* or *buoyancy aid* or *personal flotation device (PFD)* for the same reason. Few people plan to have accidents! So do not worry about the expected, but prepare for the unexpected. Because it is possible to drown in a few inches of water if you are facedown and unconscious, no lake is too small for life jackets. Life jackets or buoyancy aids must be worn in small sailboats at all times.

Safety Equipment

The following items of equipment should always accompany you when sailing:

1. Life jackets. Everyone should wear one. Although sailing has one of the most accident-free records of all sports, when dealing with something as unpredictable as the wind, caution is sensible. A good life jacket/buoyancy aid/PFD should allow complete freedom of movement, be lightweight, and not chafe the skin. When buying one, make sure it is right for your size and weight. Because you may have to duck suddenly under the boom, check that your life jacket allows you to bend easily at the waist and that it has nothing around the neck that could catch on the boom. Make sure all fastenings are noncorrosive and easy to use—even when your fingers are cold and not nimble enough to manipulate small, intricate parts. Most small-boat sailors prefer the vest type, which keeps them afloat, but it is not designed to keep the head out of the water if a person is unconscious. To get this extra protection, sacrifice a lit-

Figure 5-1 A milk container bailer

tle to bulk and mobility and get one with a cushion behind the neck, with the majority of the buoyancy in front of you. Many countries have national authorities that give approval to life jackets, so look for a Coast Guard [or Ship and Boat Builders] seal of approval or recommendation.

2. A scoop or bailer of suitable size. An empty plastic milk container can be cut to provide an inexpensive scoop (see Figure 5-1).

3. A paddle or oars. In a few unusual cases (e.g., if the mast has broken), sailing after a capsize may not be possible; therefore, always carry an alternative form of propulsion in any boat such as a motor for a large yacht and oars for a small outboard motorboat. If you forget your paddle, your centerboard can be pressed into service.

4. A *painter*. This length of rope, attached to the boat at the bow, should be at least as long as your boat. You may use it to moor your boat or as a tow rope.

General Safety Rules

Even though you should always wear a life jacket or buoyancy aid, you should also be able to swim. If the boat tips over and *capsizes*, you will sometimes get thrown clear of the

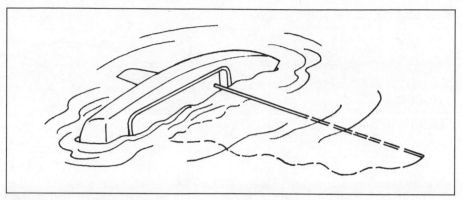

Figure 5-2 A capsized boat

boat and must swim back to her. As a general rule, always stick with your boat because rescuers can spot her more easily than your head bobbing in the water. Do not attempt to swim to shore. Virtually all modern small sailboats can be righted after a capsize and sailed, and the shore is always much further away than it looks. If you are in constant fear of capsizing because you cannot swim, your rate of learning to sail will be much slower than if you were confident in the water. As a guide, you should be able to swim a minimum of 100 yards without difficulty and be able to tread water for 5 minutes. If you are able to pass these tests without wearing a life jacket, then when wearing one your confidence should be even greater. In fact, a capsized boat is usually extremely buoyant, and the crew members need only to hold onto her to remain above water.

Procedures When Capsized

Capsizing is probably what novice sailors worry about the most. Undoubtedly, you will get wet, but you are most unlikely to be hurt falling into the water. Because capsizing is a natural part of small boat sailing, make it happen to you deliberately the first time you sail so you are not taken by surprise. An intentional, practice capsize in a warm, confined pool or inlet is an ideal situation in which to learn what to do. Alternatively, see if you can persuade an experienced friend to take you sailing and capsize with you.

A capsize occurs when the wind strength suddenly changes and the crew members either do not or cannot react in time to adjust the sail or their positions in the boat. Usually this occurs when the wind strength suddenly increases and the boat tips over onto the leeward or sail side. However, a capsize can also occur to the windward or nonsail side if the wind strength suddenly decreases and if there is too much crew weight to windward. A capsize to leeward can usually be avoided by (a) leaning out hard from the boat away from the sail into the wind, (b) allowing the sheet to run out so that the sail flaps, or (c) heading the boat into the wind so the sail flaps. If you sense you are about to capsize, your natural reaction in your anxiety will probably be to take a tight grip of the sheet and tiller. Unfortunately, this may contribute to the certainty of the capsize! Fight this reaction and release the sheet instead. A capsize to windward is best avoided by making sure you can get your weight inboard as quickly as you can hike out.

A capsized boat will either be on her side as in Figure 5-2 or might turn turtle to the position shown in Figure 5-3.

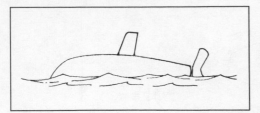

Figure 5-3   A turtled boat

Figure 5-4   Righting a turtled boat

Here is a checklist of what to do after a capsize. Learn the points thoroughly so that you can recite them from memory.

1. Check that all members of the crew are above water and with the boat.

2. Check that none of the equipment is floating away; everything should have been tied in! Do not swim more than a few feet from the boat to retrieve equipment. You can always sail to pick it up after you right the boat.

3. If the boat has turned turtle, first get her to the position shown in Figure 5-2 by exerting pressure on one corner of the boat (see Figure 5-4).
    Next, orient the boat so that the bow is pointing into the wind. If you are unable to tell the wind direction, hold the boat from the bow and you will act like a sea-anchor. In time the boat will be blown into the correct position, pointing into the wind.

4. Check that the centerboard is pushed all the way down through the boat so that as much as possible protrudes to what would normally be underneath the boat.

5. Swim to the protruding end of the centerboard, and lever the boat upright by pushing down hard on the centerboard (see Figure 5-5).
    If you have the strength, raise yourself up on top of the centerboard, for this makes righting the boat easier. Because a longer lever generates more force than a shorter one, lean out away from the hull, but be careful not to break the centerboard by putting all of your weight too near the tip. This righting procedure takes a few seconds. Because the sail sometimes seems to "stick" to the water surface, the first few degrees of righting the boat are the most critical and take the most effort.

6. With the boat upright, clamber aboard somehow. Grace and style are not important in this maneuver, which varies according to boat type. You may find it easier to clamber in over the stern or over the side. Ask your fellow crew members to help keep the boat stable to avoid repeating the capsize.

7. Check that everything is in place and then proceed. Some emptying out of water, or *bailing*, may be needed in some boats; others have automatic draining devices.

Try using the following cue as a memory aid for what to do when capsized: *SAILBAG*—what a sail is stored in.

Figure 5-5   Righting a capsized boat

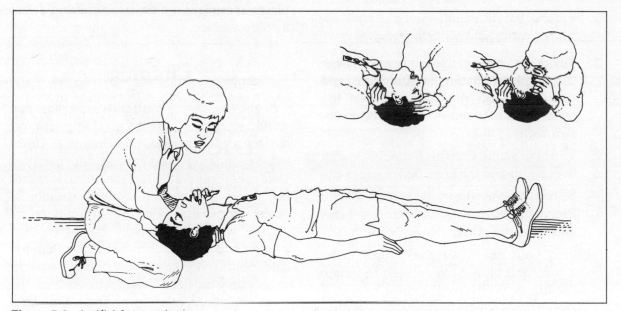

Figure 5-6   Artificial resuscitation

Sailors safe
All secured
Into wind
Lengthen 'board
Boat upright
All aboard
Get out water

Artificial Resuscitation

Another skill you must know but hope never to have to use is artifical resuscitation, or breathing for someone else who has stopped breathing (see Figure 5-6).

If you suspect someone is in need of

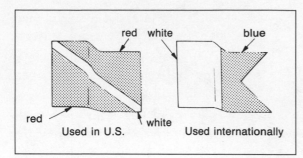

red white   blue

red

Used in U.S.   Used internationally

Figure 5-7   Diving flags

artificial resuscitation, take the following action:

1. Check for breathing. Do not assume you *must* give artificial resuscitation, but if the victim is not breathing, start resuscitation *immediately*. Every second counts.

2. Turn the victim onto his or her face to drain any water out of the mouth.

3. Turn the victim onto his or her side, clear the mouth and throat of obstructions, and strike hard on the back between the shoulder blades to dislodge any other obstruction.

4. Turn the victim onto his or her back. Pull the jaw up and the head back to open the airway.

5. Pinch the victim's nose with one hand and hold the jaw firmly with the other.

6. Place your mouth over the victim's, make a seal, and blow hard enough to inflate the lungs. Watch for the chest to rise. If the victim is a baby or child, blow gently.

7. Repeat breaths about 20 per minute, until the victim is breathing by him- or herself, or until help arrives. Keep checking that breathing has continued.

8. Keep the victim warm.

Steps 1-6, the initial check to getting in the first, vital breath, should take no more than 10 seconds. Never give up hope; some vic-

tims have made full recoveries after having been resuscitated for several hours.

If a mannequin is not available for practice, two people can run through the drill but should blow to the side of the "victim's" head and *not* into the mouth.

Diving Flags

For safety's sake, you must be able to recognize the diving flag (see Figure 5-7).

In the United States, this is a red oblong flag with a white diagonal slash. All other countries use International Code Flag A, a white and blue vertically halved flag, with the blue part being swallow-tailed. The warning flag is flown to indicate to people on the surface that divers are in the area. Do not sail in such places because of the danger of hitting divers as they surface.

Clothing

Beginning sailors naturally ask what they should wear. Shoes with a good grip on a wet surface are essential. Other than that, clothing depends on the weather and personal taste. Shorts and a T-shirt are fine in summer but waterproof clothing should usually be taken along in case of need. The temperature on the water will usually be lower than ashore, and it is better to be too hot than too cold. Some sailors wear wet suits for warmth in case they capsize. This makes sense on the open sea where, even in summer, the water temperature can be cold, quickly robbing the body of heat. Although it does provide some buoyancy, a wet suit should never be substituted for a life jacket/buoyancy aid/PFD.

Enough of theory. Now it is almost time to sail. Check your understanding of the material in this chapter with the following questions, and then take the test on part 1. Reread any sections in which you did not do well and always try to visualize the real situation. And, if any experienced sailor offers to take you sailing, say yes!

Questions on Chapter 5

1. Explain the following terms:
   (a) painter (b) capsize to leeward (c) capsize to windward (d) bailing.

2. What should always be (a) worn and (b) taken on every sail? For each answer, explain why.

3. Explain three actions you can take while sailing to reduce the chance of capsizing to leeward.

4. What is the most usual cause of capsizing to windward?

5. Explain exactly what to do in the event of a capsize, and for each action you mention, give the reason why this is done.

6. Explain what steps you would take to resuscitate someone who doesn't appear to be breathing.

7. What does a red flag with a white diagonal slash or blue and white halved flag with swallowtail at blue end indicate?

Activities for Chapter 5

1. Check out your swimming ability.

2. Ask an experienced sailor to take you sailing and capsize the boat on purpose.

3. Practice artificial resuscitation in teams of two. Make sure you breathe to the side of the ''victim's'' mouth in practice.

Test Yourself on Part 1

1. Point to the following on a diagram or, better yet, on the boat you will sail:

   (a) tiller (b) port side (c) sheet (d) boom (e) halyard (f) bow (g) luff of sail (1 point each; 7 points total.)

2. What three actions can be taken when sailing to prevent a capsize? (1 point each; 3 points total.)

3. List the following in the order of actions you would take following a capsize:

   (a) Point the boat into the wind.

   (b) Lever the boat up using the centerboard.

   (c) Check that all is secured.

   (d) Check that each member of the crew is safe.

   (e) Clamber aboard.

   (f) Remove water from the boat.

   (g) Check that the centerboard is pushed all the way through the boat. (7 points total; deduct 1 for each wrong order)

4. Give three accurate methods of finding the wind direction. Do them. Do you get the same answer each time? (1 point each; 3 points total.)

5. List the following in the order of actions you would take to rig a boat stored ashore:

   (a) Hoist the mainsail.

   (b) Launch the boat stern first.

   (c) Hoist the jib.

   (d) Point the boat into the wind.

   (e) Check that life jackets are being worn and paddles and bailer are on board. (5 points total; deduct 1 for each wrong order)

6. You are on a reach and your sail flaps. Explain two ways to stop the flapping. (1 point; 2 points total)

7. How can you stop a boat moving forward? When might you use this principle? (1 point each part; 2 points total)

8. You try to come about but get stuck half way, pointing into the wind. What is the most likely cause? How can you get going again? (1 point each part; 2 points total)

9. What is the single most important aspect of artificial resuscitation? (1 point)

Scores:

32-30 Excellent. Sailing is in your blood!
29-25 Good. Just a few points to clear up.
24-20 Fair. Try rereading the chapters.
Below 20 Poor. Do not give up. Ask your instructor or other sailors to go over the points you missed; then reread the chapters and retake the test.

Now, on to part 2 and the water!

Part 2
Practical Skills

6

The First Sail: Reaching, Coming About, and Docking

The big moment is here: your first sail! Be sure to pick good weather conditions, and give yourself plenty of time to have a lot of fun.

Objectives

- To determine if conditions are safe for you to sail
- To sail a boat back and forth on reaches
- To make the boat come about
- To return safely to your launch point
- To answer the questions on p. 52

Helpful Terms

To make fast. To secure.

Sternway. Backward movement of the boat.

Determine Sailing Conditions

If you are learning to sail in a class, your instructor will determine when conditions are right for your first sail. If you are on your own, you must decide for yourself. Here are the points you need to consider.

Obviously, you'll want to sail on a warm day that will remain so; therefore, listen to weather forecasts. Plan to arrive at your sailing site early so that you do not feel pressured by time. Check for other boats of approximately the same size as yours that will be sailing and watch how they are faring. Because you might need help, you certainly don't want the place to be deserted, but because you will need plenty of room to maneuver, you don't want the water to be too crowded either.

Wind Strength

The most critical factor for your first sail is the wind, both its strength and direction. A slight breeze—enough to keep a flag moving but not enough to blow it out horizontally—is ideal. Another way to test if the wind is too strong is to see if you can paddle your boat against the wind, as you might have to do in an emergency. If you can't, do *not* go out. If you are not fortunate enough to have a friend or instructor sail near or with you, make sure of two things:

(a) That someone is constantly watching you from the shore, and

(b) That you keep close to your launch point so that you can paddle back comfortably if necessary.

Wind Direction

First, determine the wind direction (see p. 10). If you are sailing on a large expanse of water and cannot easily see the opposite shore, or if you are on the open sea and the wind is blowing off the land, *do not sail*. If you get into difficulties under these circumstances, you would be blown further and further away from help.

Check Equipment

Gather all your equipment together in the boat and make sure the boat is pointed into the wind. Rig your boat (see p. 32) (without the jib if you are alone) and do not be afraid to ask others for help. There's a first time for everyone. If your boat has a hiking stick [tiller extension], fold it back onto the tiller and fix it there temporarily with a rubber band. Use a hiking stick only in windy conditions when you must hike out.

Run through these checks before getting under way:

(a) Is everyone on board wearing a life jacket?

(b) Are paddles, oars, or a motor on board?

(c) Is a scoop/bailer on board?

(d) Is someone who knows your plans keeping an eye on you?

(e) Are all the knots/cleatings *made fast* (secured)?

Practical Exercise 1: Sailing on Reaches

Your goals in this first sail, apart from having a good time, are to launch the boat, to sail back and forth on reaches, to come about each time you turn, and to return safely to the shore. If ever you feel the need to take a ''time-out'' while sailing on a reach, you have only to let the sheet out and allow the sail to luff. When you are ready to sail again, pull in the sheet, and you will be off.

Before you go out, run through the land drill for coming about once again, using the props suggested on p. 19. Remember that your goal is to reach, or to move at 90° to the wind's direction with the sail halfway out so that before you come about, you must head up the boat and sail briefly in a close-hauled or beating position. First, pull in the sail hard. Then alter course to 45° to the wind by pushing the tiller slightly on to the sail side, and then center the tiller. If you forget to sail first on a beat, you may end up luffing because you lacked the momentum to get around and on to the new course. If this happens, have a paddle ready to complete the turn.

Step 1—Launch

Launch your boat immediately downwind of any obstructions so that you avoid hitting them, yet have space to leeward of your launch point in which to maneuver. If the water is congested, consider paddling away from the launch area. If you have to tie up your boat or have someone hold her, she should be kept headed into the wind until you are ready to sail. If you are sailing on the ocean, leave the launching dolly [trolley] above the high-water line!

Push the centerboard down if the water is deep enough. If not, have it poised ready to be put down at the earliest opportunity. Get the rudder blade down, too. If you have a crew, the helmsperson gets in first and takes control of the tiller and the sheet, although the sheet should not yet be pulled in. If alone, you have to do this at the same time as jumping aboard. Push the boat off so you head out at 90° to the wind, or as close to that as conditions allow (see Figure 6-1).

Pull the sheet in until the sail is half in and stops flapping, get the rudder and centerboard fully down, if not already, and you are off! You should be sitting on the nonsail side, but the crew may sit on the sail side if there is not much wind. Keep the boat trimmed level fore and aft by not having too much weight at the stern. Be sure to sit in a position that

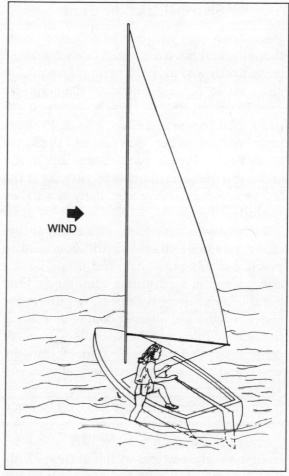

Figure 6-1 Getting under way

does not obstruct your movements of the tiller.

Step 2—Sail on Reach

The boat will try to head into the wind, so continuous small course changes with the tiller will be necessary. If the sail flaps, pull the tiller a little onto the side opposite the sail to correct this, but do not overcorrect your course. A reach course is perpendicular to the wind. If your sail is halfway out and not luffing but does luff as soon as you let it out any more, you are on exactly the right course.

Step 3—Make the Turn

As soon as you have collected your thoughts and have recovered from the fun of being under way at last, try coming about. Do not wait to come about until the opposite shoreline is crunchingly close because you will need a lot of space. Leave at least 10 times your boat length between you and the shore at all times. People who charge up to the shore intending to impress by turning at the last second may look spectacularly silly if they misjudge things.

To help you turn from one reach to the other, remember the land drill you used to practice turning the boat, and if you have a crew, give the appropriate commands. First get the boat sailing on a beat by pulling the sheet in tight and altering course by putting the tiller a little onto the sail side. Check for other boats before heading more into the wind, and continue to turn the boat until you are sailing again at right angles to the wind. If you turned correctly, then you will be headed toward your launch point.

Practice sailing on reaches back and forth in figure eight patterns as in Figure 6-2 until you become proficient and feel confident in your abilities.

Practical Exercise 2:
Returning to the Launch Point

If you have kept on course at 90° to the wind on your reaches, you should be heading back to where you launched. This is important, because once out on the water, you must also know how to return to shore. Remember to head into the wind and keep the boat headed into the wind to slow down your final approach to the leeward side of the dock. Be ready to pull up the centerboard and possibly the rudder blade when you get into shallow water.

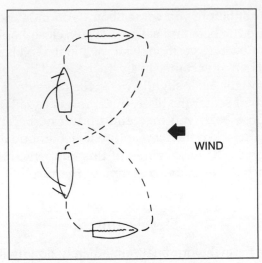

Figure 6-2 Reaching back and forth

Approaching the Dock

If you are unable to get back to your launch site, there is nothing wrong with paddling or motoring back to the starting point. Alternatively, you could land somewhere else if you are unable to make it back, and then get the sails down and paddle or pull the boat back. Wherever you land the boat, however, remember the only way to brake a sailboat is to head her into the wind and/or let out the sail.

Judging when to turn in the docking maneuver is difficult, but it is infinitely better to turn too soon and have to paddle the last few yards than it is to turn too late and hit the dock/shore with great force. That is expensive. You will find that the boat pivots around a point near her center. If possible, station a friend, perhaps the one who was keeping a check on you, to be ready to catch the boat when you return.

Docking Maneuvers

Various wind directions and appropriate docking maneuvers are shown in Figure 6-3.

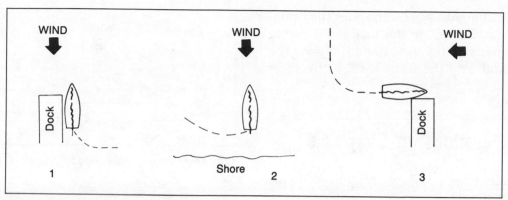

Figure 6-3 Docking maneuvers

Note that in Situation 2, you head into the wind, stop, and float backward to the launch site. Whenever a boat is going backward or has *sternway*, the tiller controls are reversed. If you want the bow to turn to port, push the tiller to port. This is because the flow of water past the rudder is moving in the opposite direction to normal.

Whenever you secure your boat with the painter, allow her a few feet of rope on which to swing with the slight wind changes. Make certain she really is secured and that she will not bump other boats or anything else when she does swing.

Checkpoints for Reaching, Coming About, and Docking

1. Did you have difficulty knowing how far in or out the sail should be on a reach? The problem might be

    (a) having the sail out too far. You know this is your problem if the sail luffs.

    (b) having the sail in too far. This cannot be seen, but you can test for this problem by letting the sail out a little. It should start to luff immediately.

2. Did you have difficulty knowing when you were headed on a reach? Check for this by

    (a) setting the sail half out and turning the boat until the sail just stops luffing;

    (b) looking at the wavelets. A reaching boat will be sailing parallel with the wavelets.

3. Did you have difficulty turning the boat without getting stuck in irons? The most common errors are

    (a) trying to come about from a reach without first heading up to a beat and sailing on that course for a few seconds.

    (b) centering the tiller too soon. Keep it across until the sail has begun to fill on the new course.

4. Did you have difficulty docking?

    (a) If you approached too quickly, head up into the wind sooner. The boat's momentum will carry her forward a while.

    (b) If you failed to reach the dock, paddle the last few feet.

5. Did you find that the turn happened too quickly?

    Be certain to turn the bow into the wind; you may have been gybing.

6. Did you feel your body was twisted when you were steering?

Check that you were sitting on the opposite side to the sail. In this position of facing across the boat, the back hand is always the tiller hand, and the front hand is the sheet hand.

Questions on Chapter 6

1. Under what conditions might you decide not to sail?

2. (a) On what course should you sail briefly before attempting to come about?

   (b) Why?

3. (a) To which side of a dock or obstacle should you sail?

   (b) Why?

4. What factors must you consider when docking your boat? Indicate how each factor would affect your actions.

5. If you find yourself unable to get back to your launching point under sail, what can you do to get back?

Activities for Chapter 6

1. Set out two buoys about 100 yards apart so that a line between them is at right angles to the wind. Reach from one buoy to the other, head up, and come about

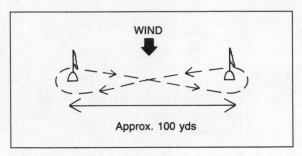

Figure 6-4   Buoy arrangement for chapter 6, Activity 1

around it as in Figure 6-4. Repeat several times.

2. Have your friend ashore blow a whistle at frequent intervals. The sound is your signal to come about as soon as you have checked that it is safe to do so.

3. Practice the "time-out" position when on a reach. Let the sails flap and wait until the boat has stopped before resuming sailing. Repeat.

4. Set the buoys up as in Activity 1. Time yourself from one buoy to the other on a reach. Multiply the time by 2. Practice controlling your boat by deliberately sailing slowly so as to arrive at the second buoy in exactly twice the time it took you before.

5. Using a buoy as your "dock," practice docking maneuvers so that you stop head to wind with your bow *exactly* at the buoy.

7

Beating, Running, and Getting Out of Irons

Now that you can sail competently on reaches, you will want to sail as efficiently in every possible direction.

Objectives

- To sail the boat on a beat and make progress upwind
- To respond with appropriate course alterations when the sail luffs
- To sail on a run without gybing accidentally
- To get the boat sailing again after being caught in irons
- To answer the questions on p. 60

Helpful Terms

Sailing by the luff. Using the luff of the sail to indicate if you are sailing on the correct course for the sail setting.

Leeway. Sideways movement of the boat.

To have way on. To be moving forward.

Practical Exercise 3: Sailing Close-Hauled/Beating

Reaching was the best direction to sail first, because as you realized, if you can reach from A to B, you can reach back from B to A. This is not true with other points of sailing. For

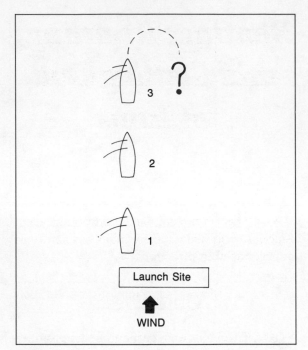

Figure 7-1   Sailing with the wind is easy, but how to return?

Figure 7-2   Start off by beating, then return downwind

example, it is tempting to steer downwind in a running direction because it seems so simple to sail this way, but it is easy to underestimate the strength of the wind on a run (see Figure 7-1).

A problem then arises when you want to return upwind because (a) you have to sail close-hauled, which is difficult to sail efficiently, (b) you cannot get there directly and have to use a zigzag course, and (c) the wind seems much stronger.

Because sailing close-hauled or beating is more difficult than running, it is most sensible to start off your second sail by trying to sail close-hauled (see Figure 7-2).

When you succeed at this, it is easy to run back. During this second sail, continue to change course as last time by pushing the tiller hard over onto the sail side and coming about, rather than by gybing.

Sailing close-hauled or beating requires great concentration, directed particularly at the sail, as well as alertness to changes in the

wind's direction. Unfortunately, the wind is almost never constant in either direction or strength. A growing sensitivity to these changes and your automatic responses to them are major factors separating the novice from the more experienced sailor. Sailing close-hauled, or as close as possible to the wind, is a constant compromise between sailing where you would like to go—into the wind—and where the wind will permit you to sail—at 45° to it. You should try to sail as close to the wind as possible without the sail luffing but not so far off this point that you are wasting time not making progress toward your upwind objective. For example, in both the diagrams of Figure 7-3 the boats are beating upwind from A to B.

In Situation 1, much time and distance is wasted because the course is never as close to the wind as possible; hence the sail can be slightly out almost on a reach setting. In Situation 2, the boat is moving forward at approximately 45° to the wind; hence this boat

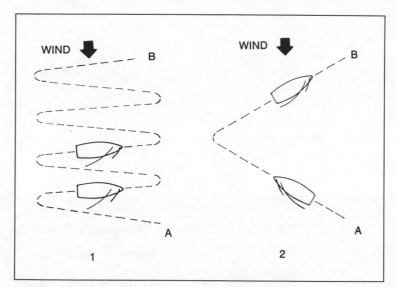

Figure 7-3 Inefficient and efficient courses upwind

Figure 7-4 Continual small alterations of course when beating

will get to B sooner than the boat in Situation 1.

Step 1—Correcting for the Wind

To sail close-hauled efficiently, first get the boat sailing on a reach, then pull the sheet in tightly, until the mainsail is pointing over the quarter, keeping the sail on the same side as when on the reach. Slowly push the tiller onto the sail side, and the boat will head up closer to the wind's direction. Do this gradually, and at the first hint of a luff in the sail—it usually shows first about halfway up the leading edge of the leading sail—pull the tiller back toward the nonsail side to fall off until the luffing disappears. Keep the sail sheeted all the way in and start to head the boat gradually up more into the wind again. As before, as soon as you notice the sail beginning to luff, alter course slightly by pulling the tiller toward you. Figure 7-4 shows exactly what you are seeking to achieve and what to avoid when sailing close-hauled.

Do not overcorrect with the tiller, or you will not be making efficient upwind progress; then you will be doing what is shown in Figure 7-3 (1). If you have a crew, ask him or her to watch out for obstructions such as other boats and the shore. You must devote your entire attention to watching the sail.

Dictated by the wind, this continual course alteration of first sailing closer to the wind, then a little less close, is called *sailing by the luff*. This means using the luff of your sail as the guide to indicate whether you are sailing as close to the wind as possible.

If you fail to react quickly enough to the sail beginning to luff and if you allow the boat to continue to turn, you will find (a) that the boat has been put about by the wind—in which case, change sides in the boat and sail on, pretending that was the place you really meant to come about anyway—or (b) that you will get stuck with the sail flapping, heading into the wind, and you will stop. You will be in irons. If this happens, either use the paddle or jerk the tiller violently to turn the boat around. Practical Exercise 5 contains more detailed information on how to get out of irons.

You must keep watching for that first little flutter in the luff of the sail and correct the boat's course to be more across the wind before the flutter progresses to full-scale flapping.

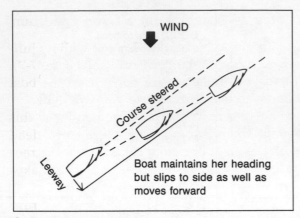

Figure 7-5 Leeway

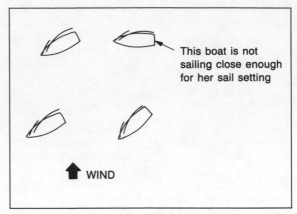

Figure 7-6   Check that you are sailing as close to the wind as others

Step 2—Being Aware of Leeway

All boats drift off to *leeward* or make some leeway when beating, even when the centerboard is all the way down. This means that as well as making forward progress, the boat also slips sideways a little (see Figure 7-5).

You should not try to steer ever closer to the wind in an attempt to counteract leeway because you will be pinching and thus sailing slowly and inefficiently. Instead, either put in an extra tack to be sure of making your destination, or figure in to your planned course the fact that you will make leeway.

Step 3—Using the Correct Sail Setting/Course Combination

When you sail too close to the wind, a flapping sail will draw your attention to the problem. It is much more difficult to know if you are not sailing close enough to the wind for your sail setting. You may, in fact, be on a reaching course relative to the wind yet still have the sheet pulled in hard. This wastes time because the sail is stalled, yet this cannot be seen by the naked eye. Other boats sailing near you can be useful guides. If they are sailing closer to the wind than you are, try heading in that direction, too (see Figure 7-6).

Another way to test whether your course and sail positions are correct with one another is to hold the course you are on and try easing the sheet out a few inches at a time. If no luffing occurs after a few inches of sheet are eased out, you have an incorrect sail setting/ course combination. You can correct this inefficient combination by doing one of two things, but do not do them both or you will be back to square one. You can either alter course and fall off to fit your sail setting, or you can alter your sail setting and pull in some sheet to fit your course. The choice you make depends on your objective. If you are concentrating on getting to a specific place quickly and efficiently, hold the best course to get there and alter your sail setting to fit the course. On the other hand, you might try to get the boat sailing as fast as possible on any particular sail setting, in which case you would first set your sails and then keep adjusting your course to keep them filled.

In summary, in good close-hauled sailing, you are always trying to find the edge of the no-go zone and remain just outside of it. Pull the sail in tight and head as close as possible to the wind until the sail begins to luff. Head the boat back the other way to just stop the luffing. Conduct a further test by holding that course and easing the sheet out a few inches;

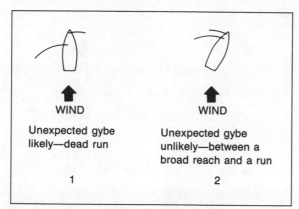

Figure 7-7 How to avoid gybing unexpectedly

if it is set correctly, the sail should flap immediately.

Eventually, you will develop a sailor's sixth sense that will tell you that the flutter is just about to appear in the sail and that you are therefore sailing close enough but can go no further. This takes time and constant experimentation to achieve. Never be afraid to experiment, but only alter one aspect at a time so that you know which one it was that made the difference.

Practical Exercise 4: Running

After sailing upwind, downwind sailing will seem simple by comparison. You might call it a breeze. Even though it will seem simple, running involves three distinct steps that must be understood and practiced.

Step 1—Letting Out the Sail

As you head your boat in the desired downwind direction, let the sail out as far as the wires supporting your mast, or shrouds, will allow, or until the sail is out at 90° to the boat. If you are truly on a run, the sail will not luff even when all the way out. If it does, alter course by moving the tiller a fraction more toward the nonsail side.

Step 2—Watching for a Gybe Condition

If your sail is all the way out with no luffing, you are on a dead run (see Figure 7-7), and you must beware not to turn the boat more to leeward, or else you will gybe.

For this reason, it is recommended at this stage that you not go completely on a dead run, as in 1, but sail a course a few degrees closer to a broad reach, as in 2. This makes an unexpected gybe much less likely.

Whenever you are close to being on a run, it's wise to keep a careful eye on the sail. If ever you see that the sail is beginning to swing across or if you feel less pull from the sheet, these are your warnings that a gybe may be imminent. If you react very quickly by pushing the tiller over onto the sail side, you may just be in time to prevent yourself from gybing, with the sail slamming from full out on one side to full out on the other side.

Step 3—Steering Out of a Run

When you are sailing on a run in a good breeze, you may feel you are going so fast that you are almost out of control. Just remember to let the tiller go onto the sail side, which it wants to do anyway, and you will head the boat up into the wind and drift to a halt. When you feel confident to get going again, use the paddle or scull around with the tiller to point the boat more across the wind.

Practical Exercise 5: Getting Out of Irons

Every sailor gets stuck in irons at some point, but it happens more often to the novice, particularly when coming about and sailing close-hauled. You already know some methods of getting your boat going again, and they are recapped here along with several more efficient methods.

Method 1—Use of Paddle

Get out your paddle and turn your boat. When you are heading across the wind, stow the paddle, center the tiller, and quickly pull in the sheet before the boat turns into the wind again.

Method 2—Use of Tiller

Because your goal in reading this book is to learn to sail a boat rather than to paddle one, you need to be able to get your boat going again without having recourse to the paddle! How you use the tiller to get out of irons depends on whether the boat is moving forward, albeit slowly, is stationary, or is drifting backward.

With way on.   If your boat is moving forward or has *way on*, you can stop the sails luffing by moving the tiller to the nonsail side. You will thus make the boat fall off. Pull in the sheet and the wind will fill your sails again.

With no way on.   If your boat has no way on but is not yet moving backward with stern-way either, a few quick jerks of the tiller will force the stern around, enabling you to get going again. You must jerk the tiller more forcefully one way than the other; otherwise, you will merely propel the boat and not turn her.

With sternway.   If your boat has sternway, you can use the tiller to turn the boat efficiently, as long as you remember that the controls are reversed. To turn to starboard, put the tiller hard across to the starboard side. Because your boat was not really designed to sail backward, be prepared to wait a few seconds for her to turn. Keep the tiller across on that same side, and when you notice the boat slipping sideways, pull the sheet in hard. At the same time, put the tiller onto the opposite side

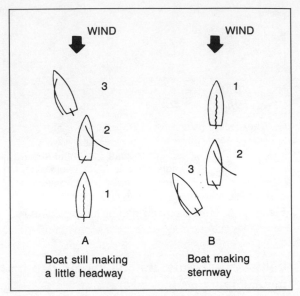

Figure 7-8   Combined use of tiller and sail to get out of irons

from before—the port side in this example—and because she is now sailing forward, she will continue to turn in the same direction. Center the tiller when the boat has gained momentum.

Method 3—Use of Tiller and Sail Combined

The most efficient method of getting out of irons is to use a combination of tiller and sail movement. Force the boom halfway out to one side (e.g., to starboard) until the whole sail catches the wind and the boat will swing to port.

If the boat has way on, putting the tiller to the sail side will help as in Figure 7-8 A; if the boat has sternway, putting the tiller to the nonsail side will help you get out of irons more quickly as in Figure 7-8 B.

As soon as the boat has turned to a beat course, release the sail to the normal, leeward side.

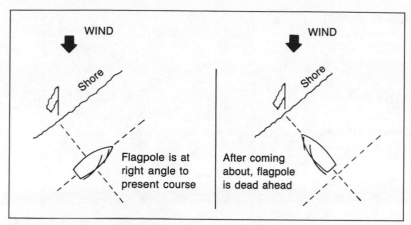

Figure 7-9 Determining where the new close-hauled course will be

Checkpoints for Beating, Running, and Getting Out of Irons

1. When beating and then coming about, did you have difficulty knowing what your new close-hauled course should be?

    When sailing close-hauled, your course is at about 45° to the wind, so when you come about, your new close-hauled course will be at about 90° to the old one (see Figure 7-9).

    To be sure of what your new course will be, first find a landmark directly abeam on the windward side. Then come about and continue to turn until your landmark is dead ahead, but do not forget that your boat will make some leeway.

2. When beating, were you unsure of when you were really on a close-hauled course?

    To ensure a close-hauled course, first pull the sheet in hard over the quarter. Then head up until the sail begins to luff; then fall off just enough to stop it luffing. This is close-hauled.

3. When beating, did you seem to be going too slowly for the windstrength? The reason(s) could be that

    (a) you were sailing too close to the wind and should fall off;

    (b) you had the sheet in too tight and should ease it out until the sail is on the point of luffing;

    (c) you did not alter your course in a windshift. Test the wind by regularly heading up and falling off.

4. Did you get caught in an unexpected gybe? To prevent this from happening again,

    (a) sail on broad reaches rather than runs;

    (b) be sensitive to the sail beginning to swing across and the pressure on the sheet lessening.

5. Did you have difficulty knowing if your boat was going forward or backward or was stationary?

    To determine this, line up two landmarks abeam. If the nearer one appears to be moving to your stern, you are moving forward; if the nearer one appears to be moving to your bow, you are moving backward; if they remain in line, you are stopped!

Questions on Chapter 7

1. What alterations do you make with the tiller and the sheet when changing from a reach to a beat?

2. (a) What is sailing by the luff?

   (b) How is it done?

3. (a) When sailing close-hauled, do you fix the course and hold it without deviating or continually alter course slightly?

   (b) Why?

4. If you sail too close to the wind, which way do you move the tiller to get back on a good close-hauled course?

5. What are the two names for sailing as close to the wind as possible?

6. What does it mean to be in irons?

7. (a) Why could it be dangerous to sail on a dead run?

   (b) How can this danger be minimized?

8. If you sense a gybe is about to occur, which way do you move the tiller to try to prevent the gybe?

Activities for Chapter 7

1. Set out two buoys about 100 yards apart, at a slight angle to the wind, as in Figure 7-10.

   Beat upwind, come about and around the buoy, and then run/broad reach down-

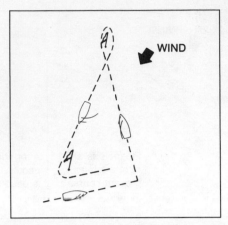

Figure 7-10 Buoy arrangement for chapter 7, Activity 1

wind. Head up around the buoy and repeat.

2. Have a friend ashore blow a whistle, and use this code:

   1 blast—sail on run
   2 blasts—sail on reach
   3 blasts—sail on beat
   4 blasts—come about

   Ask your friend to vary the sequence, but always remember to head onto a beat briefly before coming about.

3. Head on a beat until a buoy is at right angles to windward of your boat at least 100 yards away. Come about and head for the buoy. See how much leeway your boat makes. Repeat the activity, this time allowing for leeway, and see how close you can get to the buoy—without pinching!

4. Head the boat into the wind and luff. Wait at least 30 seconds and notice how the boat drifts. Get out of irons without using a paddle.

Gybing, Use of the Centerboard, and Sailing Around a Course

With the addition of the skills covered in this chapter, you can make all the basic maneuvers of sailing a small boat.

Objectives

- To gybe the boat keeping her completely under control
- To set the centerboard correctly on every point of sailing
- To sail around a triangular course that includes beating, coming about, reaching, gybing, and running
- To answer the questions on p. 66

Helpful Terms

By the lee. Sailing with the sail on the windward side; usually precedes an unexpected and violent gybe.

Leave a buoy to port/starboard. Pass by a buoy so it is to your left/right.

Practical Exercise 6: Gybing

Perhaps by this time you have already gybed by mistake, or tried it anyway, and survived. The key to successful gybing is to keep the boat under control at all times.

Before you try gybing on the water, run through the land drill again, using the props suggested on p. 19.

Step 1—
Choose Calm Conditions and a Broad Reach/Run Course

When you are out on the water, choose a calm, gust-free moment for your first gybe. Sometimes the water and wind are much calmer behind an island or other obstruction.

Sail the boat on a course between a broad reach and a run while you are preparing to gybe. This is because when you are on a true run, the wind has only to change slightly to the old leeward side of your boat and you will be sailing *by the lee* (see Figure 8-1).

This means that the sail is now, briefly, on the windward side—the wrong side! Unless you react quickly at this point, a sudden, uncontrolled and unexpected gybe will occur, and the boom will crash across from full out one side to full out the other side. The momentum of this can be enough to capsize a small boat.

Step 2—Zigzag Downwind

A good way to practice gybing is to zigzag downwind. This way you can gybe every 30 seconds or so to make gybing as smooth an operation as possible (see Figure 8-2).

Remember the land drill you used for gybing, and if you have a crew, give the appropriate commands. First pull in the sheet until the sail is half in, then turn onto a true run. Check that the sheet will be free to run out quickly after the boom has swung across. As with coming about, always check carefully to ensure that there is space for you to turn before you start, as you would check a car's rearview mirror before changing lanes. Only now do you pull the tiller across. Be sure to center the tiller as the boom swings across to maintain control, and let the sheet run out. Sail onto your new broad reach/run course and repeat this maneuver until you are confident that you have the boat completely under control.

Remember that if you feel it is too windy to gybe, you can always avoid it by going the long way around and coming about as in Figure 8-3. There is nothing wrong with doing this, and if it makes you feel happier, then it is certainly the correct thing to do.

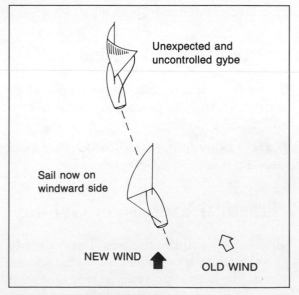

Figure 8-1 Sailing by the lee

Figure 8-2 Practicing gybing by zigzagging downwind

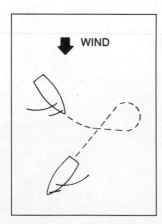

Figure 8-3 Avoiding gybing

Practical Exercise 7: Using the Centerboard

You are capable of sailing from anywhere to anywhere, so the next step is to improve your efficiency on all points of sailing. One way you can do this is to start sailing with a jib, if your boat has one. All boats, however, will sail more efficiently if you adjust the centerboard correctly for each point of sailing.

Step 1—Raised on a Run

The function of the centerboard is to provide lateral resistance or to reduce the amount by which the boat tends to slip sideways on certain points of sailing. On a run, with the wind directly behind the boat, there is almost no sideways thrust, so the centerboard does nothing to stop this nonexistent thrust. In fact, by being down in the water, the centerboard is actually slowing you on a run because of the drag or resistance it offers. Thus you should raise the centerboard to help the boat go faster on a run. The only occasion when the board might not be raised all the way on a run would be in rolling waves when a little

centerboard can be kept down to reduce the rolling effect on the boat.

Step 2—Down on a Beat

In the opposite extreme to a run, which is a beat, the boat uses the centerboard to achieve a sailing course of around 45° to the wind. The centerboard must be all the way down or else the boat will slip off to leeward and sail most inefficiently (see Figure 8-4).

Step 3—Halfway on a Reach

In between these two courses, on a reach, it might seem at first glance as if the centerboard would be most useful here; but it is not required to work quite so hard at transferring a sideways or forward of sideways wind into headway on a reach as on a beat. Clearly, however, there is more likelihood of slipping sideways on a reach than on a run, so the board is positioned about halfway up on a reach for the best possible combination of factors. This is easy to remember if you match a half-out sail, a reach, with a half-out-of-the-water centerboard. Likewise, when the sail

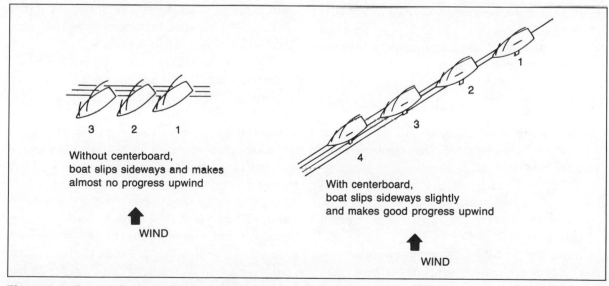

Without centerboard, boat slips sideways and makes almost no progress upwind

WIND

With centerboard, boat slips sideways slightly and makes good progress upwind

WIND

Figure 8-4 Reason for centerboard being down on a beat

is pulled all the way in on a beat, the centerboard should be all the way immersed in the water; and on a run with the sail all the way out, the centerboard should be all the way out of the water. Never remove it altogether, however, in boats where this is possible, because you might need to put it down again in a hurry should you need to alter course quickly.

Naturally, any "in-between" sail setting is matched with an in-between centerboard setting. If you are in any doubt about the correct position of the centerboard, experiment. Try beating with the centerboard up, and notice how you slip sideways or make leeway. Then hold your course and put the board down and feel the change in how the boat is sailing. Note, also, how the heading changes.

Practical Exercise 8: Sailing Around a Course

Now that you can sail in all directions, you will probably enjoy the challenge of being set a specific course to sail. The transition from sailing anywhere, on a whim, to sailing a prearranged course with specific goals to attain and round should be quite easy. However, you must be more aware of all factors, such as wind changes, so that you can keep going where you need to instead of where you happen to be blown.

Step 1—Triangular Course

A simple type of course to sail is a triangular course. A well-chosen triangular course will let you try out your skills in beating, reaching, and broad reaching/running, as well as coming about and gybing. As you know by now, the beat is the most difficult point of sailing to sail well.

Because the beat best sorts people out, racing courses are usually set so that a beat comprises the first leg of the course. This prevents everyone who set off at the same time from arriving together at the first buoy. Think of the chaos if 50 boats all tried to round a buoy simultaneously! The second leg of the course is often a reach, followed by a downwind leg back to the starting area.

The layout of a typical course is shown in Figure 8-5. A to B is the beating, or close-hauled leg. If there are 20 boats sailing, there could be 20 possible courses from A to B. Two extreme examples are shown, one with many short tacks and one with just two long ones. (For a consideration of what path to take, see chapter 11.) B to C is a reach and boats will sail a straight line here. C to A is also straight and note that at C boats will gybe in order to take the quickest route back to A.

The instructions you would receive for this course might be A to B to C to A, keeping outside all the buoys in a clockwise direction. More nautically, this would be stated as *leaving* all buoys to starboard, which means you must pass them so they are on the right side of your boat.

Step 2—Triangle and Sausage Course

There are, naturally, other course variations. Olympic-type racing courses use what are called "triangles and sausages" (see Figure 8-6) because this maximizes the number of beating legs in a race.

If you are in a class, your instructor will set you a course. If you are alone, set your own course. At first, just pick out several points and then stick to the plan until you have completed the course you set yourself. Once you can do that, spend a little time planning a course for yourself that will incorporate a beat, a reach, a gybe, and a downwind leg. To do this, first make sure you know the wind direction. From your designated starting place, find a point directly into the wind that will be your upwind buoy. From there, choose another point to reach at right angles to the wind. Gybe around this point sail back to

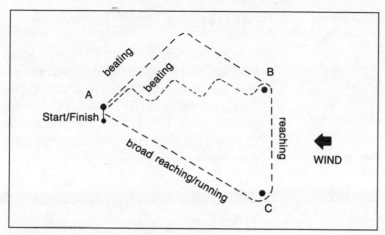

Figure 8-5 Layout of typical course

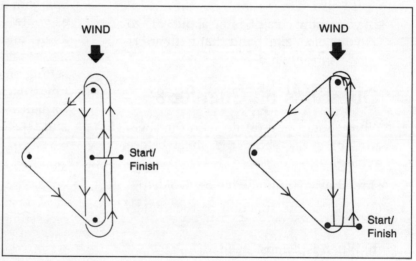

Figure 8-6 Olympic-type courses

your starting point, and continue a second lap of your course. When you actually sail your course, check to see if you were accurate in your course setting.

Checkpoints for Gybing, Use of the Centerboard, and Sailing Around a Course

1. Did you have difficulty avoiding sailing by the lee?

It is easy to avoid if you

(a) sail at a slight angle to the wind, between a broad reach and a run;

(b) immediately push the tiller slightly away from you if you feel the pressure on the sheet lessen.

2. Did the boom swing across very violently when you gybed? The reason(s) could be

(a) not pulling in some sheet before you gybed;

(b) gybing in a gust.

3. Did the boat swing violently and almost or actually capsize when you gybed? The reason(s) could be

   (a) failing to let the sheet out smoothly after the boom swung over;

   (b) failing to center the tiller as soon as the boom swung over;

   (c) failing to balance the boat adequately after the boom swung over.

4. Did you have trouble sailing around a course? If so, it was probably on the beating leg. Next time, check that

   (a) the sail was pulled all the way in over the quarter;

   (b) your new "zag" is at about 90° to your old "zig," and that both are at 45° to the wind.

Questions on Chapter 8

1. What should you (a) do with the sheet and (b) check about the sheet before gybing?

2. How may gybing always be avoided?

3. (a) What is the function of the centerboard?

   (b) When is it most needed?

   (c) When is it least needed?

4. (a) When the sail is half out, what is the most efficient centerboard setting?

   (b) Why?

5. Draw an efficient, exact path that you might take if you received the following instructions: A to B to C to A, leaving all buoys to port.

C •

B •

A •

Activities for Chapter 8

1. Set out two buoys about 100 yards apart so that a line between them is at right angles to the wind. Reach from one to the other, fall off, and gybe around it. Repeat several times. This is the same drill as you did with coming about, only now you are turning the other way.

2. Set out a series of buoys in line with the wind, about 20 yards apart. Start at the upwind end and "slalom" through between the buoys on broad reaches, gybing as you zigzag.

3. Sail with another boat of the same type as yours. Decide on a course with a triangle and a sausage. One boat will deliberately have an incorrect centerboard setting on each leg of the course. Notice how this incorrect setting affects the performance of your boat. Switch over roles and repeat.

4. As an alternative to Activity 3, if you are alone, time yourself around your chosen course with incorrect centerboard settings at all times. Then sail the course with correct settings and see how much faster you can sail the course.

5. Try your hand at synchronized sailing. You will need at least two boats but can include as many as you want. Use either music or whistle signals and work out a short routine that involves all points of sailing, and both coming about and gybing. Why not include a capsize!

9

Heavy and Light Weather Sailing; Man-Overboard Drill

Changes in wind strength provide one of the basic variables of sailing. When the wind is extremely strong or light, you should use different techniques to get the best out of your boat.

Objectives

- To know what adjustments to make in heavy weather
- To know what adjustments to make in light weather
- To successfully complete the man-overboard drill
- To answer the questions on p. 74

Helpful Terms

Heavy weather sailing. Sailing in strong winds.

Light weather sailing. Sailing in light breezes.

Outhaul. Rope on the boom to adjust the tension of the foot.

Reef. To reduce the sail area by rolling or folding at the foot.

Hiking straps. Straps to hold your feet so that you can hike out.

Spill wind.   To deliberately allow wind out of the sail.

Sit in.   To bring one's weight back into boat; opposite of hiking out.

Planing.   Sailing fast enough for the boat to rise onto her own bow wave.

Bare poles.   Mast(s) alone, no sails hoisted.

Although you now know much about how to sail a boat, you are only beginning to learn about the endless variations of the basics. Two weather variations you will encounter soon, if not already, are *heavy* and *light weather* sailing. Heavy weather sailing means sailing in strong winds and waves, and light weather sailing means sailing in light breezes and flat water. What is a strong wind? What is a light breeze? These are difficult questions because what one sailor might consider ''heavy'' or ''light'' conditions might not be so considered by another sailor. Each set of conditions, however, calls for its own skills, developed over hours of practice.

Heavy Weather Sailing

Experienced small-boat sailors define heavy weather as wind blowing above Force 4. (See the Beaufort Scale in Appendix A for a chart of wind force and water conditions.) Heavy weather, however, for the novice sailor may begin once *any* white caps form on the water or even before. Sailing has a good safety record, but the wind can create dangerous conditions, and you must not underestimate the destructive power of wind and waves. Other things to consider are the character of the wind (steady or gusty), the direction of the wind (onshore or offshore), the state of the water (choppy or flat), the place where you are planning to sail, the weather forecast, and your boat. After considering these factors, use the following points to help you make your own decision about whether to sail:

1. Recognize that the decision to sail is yours; do not be pressured by others and feel you should go out just because they are. Sometimes it takes more courage to say no than to follow the crowd blindly.

2. Do not go out at all in heavy conditions unless you are certain you are proficient enough to deal with any situation that might arise. Consider where help would come from if you needed it. If no other boats are in the area, do not sail.

3. If in doubt, stay ashore. A thrill of excitement is typical in such conditions but when that gives way to doubt or fear, it is time to stay ashore or come in.

4. If the U.S. Coast Guard or other authority displays warning signals (i.e., a red triangular flag) indicating that conditions are not safe to sail, obey the signals. (Other countries' coast guards may display gale warning signals, usually black, pointed cone shapes.)

5. At the slightest chance of a thunderstorm, do not sail. Lightning is attracted to tall metal points, and your mast would make a perfect target.

If you make the decision to sail, then as a general rule, everything that can be adjusted should be hauled in tightly for heavy conditions. Halyards must be hauled extra tight and be well secured because they will try to work loose. If your sail has *outhaul* adjustments or ropes that adjust the foot of the sail at either or both ends of the boom and/or a boom vang, these should be tightened to make the sail flatter. Sheets, however, still require adjusting according to your point of sailing and must *never* be cleated in a small boat in case of a sudden gust. If you can reduce the sail area by *reefing*, do so before setting out. (See p. 70 for how to reef.)

If you are in doubt about whether any fitting is secure enough, either replace it or do not go out.

Figure 9-1 Hiking far out

Practical Exercise 9: Hiking Out and Sitting In

Sailing in heavy weather can be enjoyable for more experienced sailors who have learned to make adjustments to gusting winds. The following hints on hiking and reacting to the wind will help you to prepare for sailing in heavy winds.

Step 1—Use Hiking Straps

In heavy weather your boat will lean much more than usual, so you must work hard to keep her upright. You and your crew will probably have to hike well out opposite the sail, and if your boat has *hiking straps* [toestraps], use them to allow you to lean out even further. Practice leaning out so far that you get the back of your head wet (see Figure 9-1).

The helmsperson should use the hiking stick [tiller extension] to help him or her lean out further. At first you may be reluctant to sit well out because you feel insecure about sitting almost out of the boat; however, you will develop this skill gradually as your confidence in the boat grows and as you sail in windier conditions. Always aim to sail the boat as upright as possible because it's faster than sailing a boat heeling over several degrees.

Step 2—React to the Wind

If the wind becomes too strong for you to handle, you may need to deliberately allow wind to escape from the sails by *spilling wind* from your sails. This can be done in two ways: Either sail with the sails slightly too far out all the time so that you heel less because the sails luff slightly; or if a particularly ferocious gust hits, head up into the wind briefly and luff.

Heavy weather makes sheets harder to hold tight, but the mainsheet should on no account be cleated. To do so is to invite a capsize in a gust.

After several gusts, you will rapidly become adept at leaning out backward to counteract their force; however, you must be equally prepared to quickly get your weight back inboard again at the end of the gust. This is called *sitting in*.

If you fail to react to this sudden reduction in wind strength quickly enough, you will probably tip the boat over and capsize to windward because you had too much weight out on the windward side. You usually end up under the sail, which is not particularly pleasant, but you can always breathe in the air pocket under the sail. Right the boat as on p. 39.

Adjusting to Waves and Gusts

In strong wind and waves try to come about as little as possible because every time the boat is head to wind, she is pushed backward.

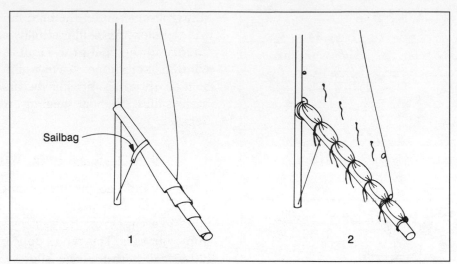

Sailbag

1   2

Figure 9-2 Methods of reefing

Start to tack when the bow has just gone over the top of a wave so you are not stopped dead by one, and keep going as fast as possible throughout the maneuver. In heavy weather it is likely that the strength of the wind will catch you in irons unless you keep up your speed. Gybe when moving quickly down a wave because the push of the wind is lessened by your own forward speed, and be careful to stop the boom from hitting a shroud because the force could be enough to break it. Alternatively, if necessary, avoid gybing by going the "long way around" (see p. 23).

Being on the Lookout

Be alert. Look for the signs of gusts before they hit you so you can prepare for them. Because gusts always come from the windward side, their approach is heralded by dark patches on the water, or catspaws, heading toward you. Many a capsize could have been avoided if only the crew members had had a couple of seconds to prepare themselves and the boat for the gust.

Do you remember the old expression "Keep a weather eye out"? This means keep an eye on the approaching weather. If you see dark grey or black clouds approaching, make for shelter immediately because the storm is not far away.

Reefing Sails

Some boats can have their sails reefed, or reduced in size. In some rigs this can be achieved by rolling the lower part of the sail around the boom. If this is done, some device such as a sailbag should also be rolled in so that there is still something to which to attach the vang [kicking strap]. A vang is necessary in heavy wind to keep the boom down so that the sail keeps a good shape (see Situation 1 of Figure 9-2).

Older rigs are reefed by tying reefing points or strings at the bottom of the sail around the boom in a series of square [reef] knots (see Situation 2 of Figure 9-2). In either case, the effect is to make the sail smaller; this in turn makes the boat slower but easier to keep upright. Reefing can be carried out at sea, if necessary, but it is easier to reef before starting to sail.

Trimming the Boat

Just as side-to-side balance is critical in all weather, particularly in heavy winds, so is fore-and-aft trim. When beating, the weight should be aft of normal to ease the boat over waves. On a reach, the weight should be well aft to encourage the boat to *plane*. Planing occurs in windy conditions when the boat goes quickly enough for the bow to lift slightly out of the water, with the hull skittering along the surface like a hydrofoil. The rapid increase in speed makes planing exhilarating. For a run, the weight should be amidships and spread over both sides of the boat to keep her level because a boat running in a strong wind with large waves can be very unstable. To further reduce rolling, half lower the centerboard.

Removing Sails

If conditions worsen while you are out, reduce the sail area you are fighting to control by lowering sail. You can make progress under jib alone. A boat will still move along even under *bare poles* (no sails). For this reason, never set out in a strong offshore wind. Make certain you will be blown back to safety if for some reason you cannot sail back.

Practical Exercise 10: Man-Overboard Drill

People rarely fall overboard from boats, but when it does happen, it is usually in heavy weather. You need to practice the drill so often that you can do it immediately, quickly, and efficiently under any conditions in which you consider it safe to sail. The man-overboard drill has more variations, both in theory and in practice, than practically any other sailing skill. The following method is appropriate and, above all, safe for any size of boat but is especially suited to small sailboats. From whatever point of sailing the victim falls over, this same technique is used. Review this skill regularly to be ready for

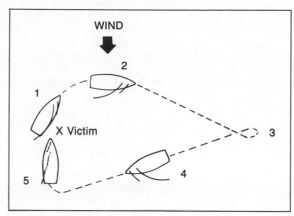

Figure 9-3 Path of man-overboard drill

the time you must use it to save someone's life (see Figure 9-3).

Step 1—Watch the Victim

As soon as a victim falls in, keep watching him or her and shout "man overboard" to alert those in your boat and in other boats nearby. Every boat needs to take action, either to avoid hitting the victim or to effect the rescue. Reassure the victim that you have seen him or her and will be back immediately; otherwise, the victim will think that you are sailing away.

Step 2—Turn to a Broad Reach

Immediately head the boat onto a broad reach, *without* either coming about or gybing. Keep watching the victim—a head bobbing in the waves is extremely difficult to relocate once lost. A broad reach is used because it ensures you can return on a reach to the victim, taking into account the fact that he or she will have floated slightly downwind in the meantime. Broad reach away for about five boat lengths. This gives you time to collect your thoughts as well as space to maneuver the boat and approach the victim correctly on your return. The windier the day, the faster the boat will move and the further away you may have to sail. Watch the victim constantly.

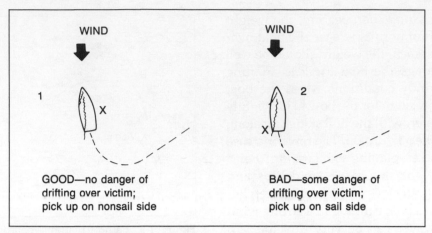

Figure 9-4 Good and bad approaches to the victim

Step 3—Come About

Turn the boat by *coming about*, remembering to sail close-hauled briefly first. Many other man-overboard drills require you to gybe here. In a small boat in windy conditions and a short-handed crew, gybing is likely to end up in a capsized boat, with no one left to rescue the man overboard. Gybing should not form part of a man-overboard drill in a small boat.

Step 4—Return on Reach

Return to the victim on a reach. Returning on a reach provides the right combination of speed and control of the boat needed to approach the victim safely. Reaching is also the easiest point of sailing.

Step 5—Head Into the Wind

Head into the wind and drift to a stop alongside the victim in exactly the same way as you would return to a dock or pick up a mooring. Always keep downwind of the victim in your approach, as in Figure 9-4 (1).

If you sail to windward, you may drift right over the victim, as in Figure 9-4 (2). The victim should be hauled in, preferably on the side opposite the sail to keep the boat balanced. If the victim is cold, tired, or

stunned and unable to help him- or herself, getting a person in such a condition aboard can be quite difficult. Using a bowline knot, tie a rope around the victim under his or her arms, and haul the victim aboard, one limb at a time.

If you misjudge your approach, go off on another broad reach in the opposite direction and reapproach the victim, as in Figure 9-5.

You must watch the victim at all times in order to make a successful rescue. Use the following aid (*WATCH*) to help you remember the different steps in the man-overboard drill:

> **W**atch and shout
> **A**way broad reach
> **T**urn about
> **C**ome back reach
> **H**ead into wind

For practice, use a dummy made from old life jackets and paddles; however, they weigh so little that it is better to use a live ''volunteer victim'' on a warm day.

Light Weather Sailing

Sailing in winds at or below about Force 2 (see the Beaufort Scale in Appendix A) is generally unspectacular with many sailors finding it dull and boring. However, light

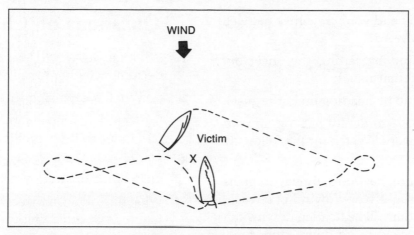

Figure 9-5 Reapproaching victim after a failed pick-up

weather sailing does require patience, particular skill, and a little luck. The ability to sit still for long periods is paramount when you are trying to sail as efficiently as possible.

The boat should be rigged with everything loose. If you have not yet rigged your jib, do so now. Every square inch of sail area helps! The sails should be baggy to help them assume an airfoil shape and be ready to use every little puff of wind. Very light winds may require both the helmsperson and crew to sit on the sail side to let gravity keep the sail to leeward and in a good shape. Alterations to course should be as infrequent as possible, because any time the rudder is turned, it causes resistance in the water and slows the boat. Any unnecessary crew movement may shake wind from the sail. The golden rule must be to keep moving forward at all costs, which may mean not sailing quite as close to the wind as usual. Also sit close to the middle or pivot point of the boat to make for faster turns and to keep the stern from dragging in the water.

Make sure that no rope nor anything else is trailing in the water. All on board must keep their weight low in the boat on upwind courses because anything sticking up above the hull will cause air resistance to forward movement. Jib sheets need to be as lightweight as possible so that the sail does not collapse under the weight of its sheets. The outer surface of the hull should be perfectly smooth on all occasions, but particularly in light airs. Hauling the boat up and sanding and/or polishing the hull surface may be worthwhile.

The wind may seem to be changing all the time in such weather. It often is. Tack only when you are certain that to do so will help you reach your objective more efficiently, but be sure to tack every time this is true.

Sailing in light weather can be extremely relaxing, provided you are not in a hurry to get anywhere. Many crews use the time to sit back and enjoy the sun and drift happily wherever the slightest breeze takes them. You should, however, always keep a good lookout.

Answer the chapter questions to check your understanding of the effects of heavy and light weather conditions on your boat.

Checkpoints for Heavy and Light Weather Sailing: Man-Overboard Drill

1. Was your boat heeling over considerably in heavy weather? To reduce the heeling angle,

(a) both you and your crew hike out well to windward;

(b) spill wind by letting the sheet out further than usual;

(c) spill wind by heading up in the gusts.

2. Did you have difficulty picking up your man overboard? Watch for the following points:

(a) Make sure that you sail away from the victim slightly downwind of a reach. The victim will be floating downwind, so you need to go downwind, too.

(b) Did you come about or gybe? Aside from being dangerous, if you gybe, you will end up downwind of the victim and have to beat back.

(c) Did you give yourself time to collect your thoughts and space to maneuver the boat?

(d) Did you head up into the wind in good time so that the boat had virtually stopped at the victim?

(e) Did you pick up the victim on the windward side of the boat so that the sail was on the other side to balance you?

3. In light winds, if you find that your boat is going much more slowly than other boats of the same type, check to ensure that

(a) the hull is as smooth as possible;

(b) you and your crew keep still;

(c) you keep the tiller centered as much as possible;

(d) nothing is trailing in the water;

(e) the sail is rigged loosely;

(f) the trim of the boat is good;

(g) you sail a little less close to the wind than usual on the beats.

Questions on Chapter 9

1. What factors would you consider when deciding whether to sail on a windy day?

2. (a) What is capsizing to windward?
   (b) What is its most common cause?
   (c) How can it be avoided?

3. How can you get advance warning of a gust about to strike you?

4. What does it mean to reef a sail? Give two methods of achieving this.

5. (a) Where should the weight of the crew be in light weather sailing?
   (b) Why?

6. In both heavy and light weather sailing, coming about should be kept to a minimum for different reasons. What are the reasons in each case?

7. Explain how you would recover a man-overboard. Why would you take each of the steps you mention?

Activities for Chapter 9

1. Every time you go to the water, estimate the strength of the wind by looking at things such as wave conditions, boats sailing, and flags. (Refer also to Appendix A.) Write down your estimate and later check its accuracy by comparing it to the newspaper/radio/TV report. With constant practice, you will soon become an accurate judge of wind strength.

2. Each day at the same time, observe and record the wind direction, and degree of cloud cover. Estimate and record the wind strength. Find out the temperature and pressure and whether the latter is rising, falling, or holding steady. Write down your forecast for the same time

tomorrow. Next day, see how accurate you were. Over a period of time, you will become more accurate at making your own local, short-term forecasts.

3. With a group of sailors, play follow-the-leader in your boats.

4. Also with a group, play Frisbee from one boat to another, calling out which boat is to collect the Frisbee next. Note that only one boat should go for the Frisbee at any one time, or else there may be some collisions!

5. In preparation for hiking out hard in heavy weather, try the following exercise on a calm day: Have your crew sit on the sail side, and you sit opposite the sail. As your crew tips the boat to leeward, you hike out hard to windward to try to get the boat upright. See if you can lean out so far that you get the back of your head wet!

6. In windy conditions, if your boat has a jib, take down the mainsail and maneuver the boat under jib alone. If you have only a mainsail that can be reefed, practice reefing on the water. If you have only a mainsail that cannot be reefed, take down your sail and see how your boat handles under bare poles.

7. In light weather, set a course and race other crews around using any method you choose—swimming, sculling, whatever you can think of. Alternatively, place limits on crews as to what actions are considered "legal" and "illegal."

10

Sailing Rules, Care of Your Boat, Ropework, and Further Knots

A knowledge of the sailing rules, a well-cared-for boat, and an efficient use of knots are hallmarks of the good sailor, whether he or she races, boardsails, or cruises. No matter what your sailing intentions, the following information will help you become a good sailor.

Objectives

- To know the basic sailing rules
- To understand how to maintain your boat in good condition
- To whip, splice, coil, and heave a line
- To tie three more knots
- To answer the questions on p. 85

Helpful Terms

Whipping. Wrapping the end of a rope to prevent it from unravelling.

Splicing. Joining the ends of two ropes by interweaving the strands.

Eye splicing. Interweaving rope strands to form an eye.

Standing part of a rope. The part under strain, usually the long section.

Bight. A hairpin type of loop in a rope.

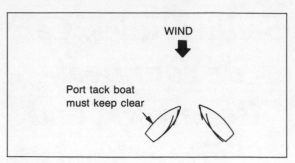

Figure 10-1 Opposite tacks right-of-way

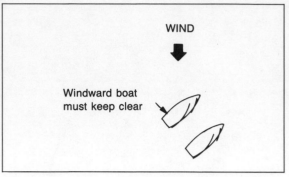

Figure 10-2 Same tack—windward/leeward right-of-way

Bitter end. The last few feet of a rope or chain close to the point of attachment on board.

Turn. To wrap rope around a solid object.

Marlinspike. A round, pointed steel tool used in ropework.

Thimble. An oval metal or plastic fitting around which the eye of a rope or wire is formed.

Sailing Rules

Having rules on the water serves the same purpose as having rules on the highway: to prevent accident and injury.

Always keep well clear of all boats so that there is no danger of collision. Although sailboats generally have right-of-way over power boats, never assume a power boat will keep out of your way. Some boats take time to maneuver, and you are asking for trouble if you get too close. A general rule of thumb is that the more maneuverable boat is expected to keep clear. Always keep a good lookout and alter course early to make your intentions obvious.

Knowledge of four basic rules should enable you to maneuver your boat with confidence in the vicinity of other boats.

The *International Regulations for Preventing Collisons at Sea*, known simply as the "Rules of the Road," state the rules for sailing vessels. In simplified form they are as follows:

1. When boats converge on opposite tacks, the one with the wind on the port side shall keep clear (see Figure 10-1).

2. When boats converge on the same tack, the one to windward shall keep clear (see Figure 10-2).

3. If a boat on port tack sees a boat to windward and cannot be certain whether the other boat has the wind on the port or starboard side, the port tack boat shall keep clear (see Figure 10-3).

4. An overtaking boat shall keep clear (see Figure 10-4).

Always be courteous, but do not assume that the other boat knows the rules. In general, if in any doubt, get out of the way.

General Care of the Boat

You will certainly want to keep your boat looking good, and the following points will help you achieve this.

Hull

Always launch and retrieve a boat with a dolly [trolley] or similar. Never pull a boat ashore or you will scratch the finish. To keep the hull smooth, brush/sponge off dirt and

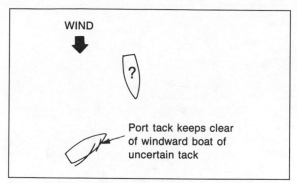

Figure 10-3 Port tack and unknown tack

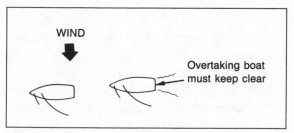

Figure 10-4 Same tack—overtaking/overtaken right-of-way

growths, and hose it down after salt water sailing. Watch for electrolysis that may occur in salt water. To prevent electrolysis, make sure that any two metal parts in contact are of the same metal; otherwise, one may dissolve away.

Use a boat cover to keep out rain and dew and also to discourage people from stealing parts from the boat. Tie down the cover securely every time you leave the boat.

Sand down and paint and/or varnish a wooden boat every 2 years or so, depending on how much the boat is used. With a fiberglass hull, use a filler paste to cover up minor blemishes, and use a fiberglass kit for major repairs. A fiberglass hull can be kept looking good with wax formulated for marine use. A boat kept afloat must be protected by antifouling paint that slows the growth of barnacles and algae.

When not in use, the boat should be kept under cover, right way up, supported on cradles if possible, and preferably in an unheated garage. If the boat has a metal centerboard, remove it or support it in place, with the weight off the boat.

Remove plugs and inspection hatches prior to storage so that air can circulate inside the boat.

Sails

Hose down or soak sails after salt water sailing, allowing them to dry before storing.

Avoid folding or bending sails repeatedly in the same place to prevent a permanent crease. Instead, coil the jib around the luff and then roll it up around the coil (see Figure 10-5).

The mainsail should be wrapped like a concertina and then rolled (see Figure 10-6).

At the end of the season, scrutinize the sails for small holes, and examine the seams for broken or chafed thread, and repair.

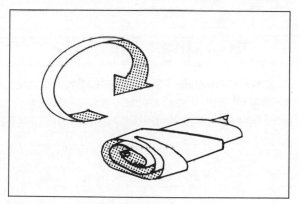

Figure 10-5 Rolling up the jib

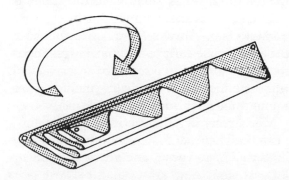

Figure 10-6 Concertina-ing the mainsail

Ropes

Before storing ropes, soak them overnight in clean, fresh water. The bathtub is a good place for this. The next day, lay the ropes out to dry. Finally, coil them as explained later in this chapter and hang them up for storage. Because some synthetic ropes deteriorate in light, store such ropes out of direct sunlight.

Spars and Rigging

At the end of each season, thoroughly overhaul your spars and rigging, and make note of anything that needs mending or replacing. Look particularly for possible corrosion of metal spars and for broken strands in the shrouds. A good habit to get into is: If you are wondering whether to replace something, replace it! Store spars flat, not merely supported at each end, which may cause them to bend.

Working With Rope

An accomplished sailor usually not only sails well, but also knows how to handle rope and take care of it. Neatly coiled rope is a sign of a good sailor.

Rope Construction

For centuries, ropes—or lines as they are sometimes referred to on board—were made from natural fibers such as cotton, sisal, or manila. Sailors spent hours finishing off the ends to stop fraying and unravelling by processes called *whipping, splicing* (semipermanently joining two ropes by interweaving their strands), and *eye splicing* (making a permanent loop without using a knot).

More recently, synthetic materials have been used to make rope, including polypropylene, nylon, polyester, and kevlar. Polypropylene is generally unpopular because it is

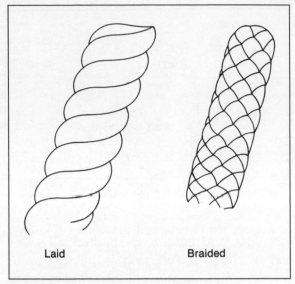

Figure 10-7 Laid and braided line

inflexible. It also floats, which could be an advantage or a disadvantage, depending on the usage. Nylon is strong and stretchy and is therefore good for mooring and tow ropes where its shock-absorbing quality is useful. Polyester products such as dacron and terylene are used for sheets and halyards because such materials do not stretch significantly. Kevlar is a new product also used to make sails. Although synthetic rope is tough and strong for its weight, it may be slippery when wet so that some knots do not hold well; plus, it can give nasty rope burns.

With the advent of synthetic materials, some of the traditional skills of rope work have less usefulness because the best way to seal the end of a synthetic rope is simply to melt it. However, many types of rope must still be cared for in traditional ways. Those traditional skills are a part of the heritage of sailing, make for better looking ropework, and can be used decoratively.

Ropes can be of either laid or braided type. Laid rope has its strands twisted together, usually in a right-handed direction. In braided rope the strands are interwoven (see Figure 10-7). The former is used for mooring lines,

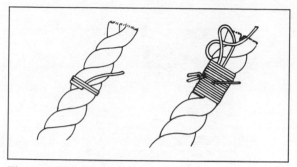

Figure 10-8 Whipping

the latter for sheets and halyards because it is less elastic, yet more comfortable in the hand, and less likely to become twisted.

Parts of a Rope

The parts of a rope, or line, include the long part away from the knot called the *standing part,* and the *bight,* or looped part, often used in making a knot. The expression "the *bitter end"* comes from the name given to the last few vital feet of an anchor rope or chain permanently attached to the boat. A *turn* in a rope occurs when it is wrapped around a solid object.

Tools Needed for Ropework

Essential pieces of equipment needed for whipping and splicing are whipping twine, which, if waxed, makes for easier work; a pair of pliers; a sharp knife; and a sharp, pointed tool known as a *marlinspike.*

Whipping

First, cut a separate 6-in. length of twine and put it on one side. Next, take three or four turns with the uncut twine around the rope about 1 to 1 1/2 in. from the end, making sure to catch the end of the twine under (see Figure 10-8).

Also check that the twine is wrapped in the opposite direction to the lay of the rope. With pliers, pull each of these turns as tightly as possible to bite into the rope. Continue taking turns with the twine until about 1/2 in. of the rope has been covered. Cut the twine with a sharp knife, leaving enough length so that 8 or 10 turns will finish wrapping the rope. Take the separate 6-in. length of twine, fold it double, and lay it along the rope. Complete the 8 to 10 tight turns, now wrapping over the 6-in. folded piece, too. One-half inch from the end of the twine, thread it through the 6-in. loop, pull it tightly around the rope for the last time, and hold it tight. Pull the 6-in. loop with the pliers so that the loop pulls the end of the whipping twine into the whipping and locks the end underneath. Neither end of the twine should be visible when you finish. Tightly done, such a piece of whipping could last as long as the rope itself, but re-whip it at the first sign of looseness because synthetic rope unravels quickly. Even if the end is melted to seal the fibers, whipping gives extra insurance against unravelling.

Eye Splicing

Eye splicing can only be done on laid rope. Make a loop at the end of the rope and tie the two sides together with twine, leaving enough free rope to form the splice (see Figure 10-9).

Also tie the individual strands tightly with twine as a temporary measure to stop them unravelling and then separate them from each other. If you plan to insert a metal inner eye, called a *thimble,* do so now. Each strand of the rope must now be tucked under its own strand in turn, and a marlinspike is used to open up the strands prior to insertion. To make this easier, color each strand differently with a felt marker and then always put the same colored strand under itself. In both eye splicing and splicing, each strand should be tucked under itself a minimum of five times.

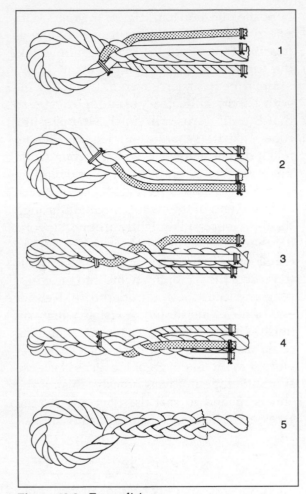

Figure 10-9 Eye splicing

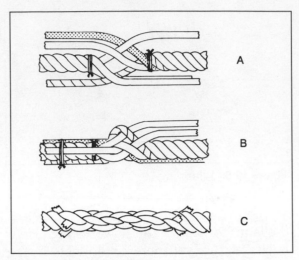

Figure 10-10 Splicing

Splicing

The principle of splicing is the same as eye splicing and again can only be done on laid rope. Tie off first to prevent unravelling and then put the two separated ends together as in Figure 10-10.

Splice one end completely and then splice the other end, turning the rope as you splice.

Coiling

No matter what size of boat you sail, you must be able to coil rope. If it is laid rope, twist it between your fingers as you coil it to stop it from tangling, and keep each coil the same length by using an arm's width for each coil (see Figure 10-11). Do not wrap it around your elbow because this gives the rope a twist.

Hanging a Coil

If the coil is not attached to anything, first coil it as before; then take a few turns around the middle of the coil with the end of the rope. Push a loop at the end through all the loops and flip it up and over the coil and pull the end tight (see Figure 10-12).

To hang up a coil attached at the end of a halyard, first coil the end as before; then reach through the coils to grasp the rope coming off the cleat, pull it through the coils, and twist it; and then hang the coil up by the end of the loop (see Figure 10-13).

Heaving a Line

Often you'll have to heave, or throw, a line to someone ashore or on another boat. First, recoil the rope to make sure the rope is not tangled. Divide the coil between your hands so that the end to be thrown, and about one third of the coil, is in your throwing hand.

Figure 10-11 Coiling

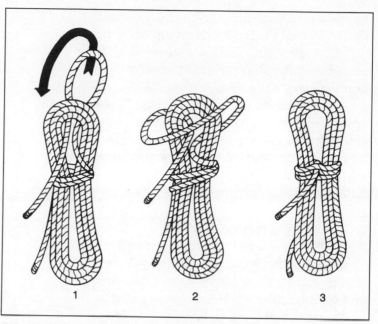

Figure 10-12 Hanging a coil—unattached

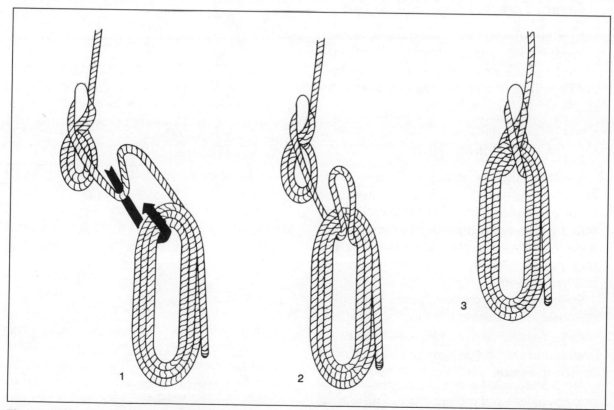

Figure 10-13 Hanging a coil—attached

Be certain to overthrow, rather than underthrow, so that the rope falls on top of the target. In a swinging motion, throw the line underhand and don't release the end in your nonthrowing hand. (see Figure 10-14).

You can also heave a line to rescue someone in the water. A bowline in the thrown end gives the victim something easy to grasp; however, make sure it really is a bowline so that it will not slip.

Figure 10-14   Heaving a line

Further Knots

Although the basic knots you will need (figure eight, clove hitch, square, bowline, and cleat hitch) have been covered in chapter 4, some other practical knots and their uses are explained here.

Round Turn and Two Half Hitches

A round turn and two half hitches, shown in Figure 10-15, may be used to tie a rope around an object such as a spar, pile, or bollard. It will hold well against low to moderate stress and is quickly tied.

Figure 10-15   Round turn and two half hitches

Rolling Hitch

A rolling hitch is shown in Figure 10-16. This is a good knot for taking hold against a stress parallel to the object around which it is tied because it tightens under strain. The arrows on Figure 10-16 indicate the direction of the pull.

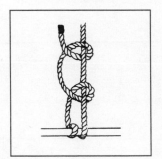

Figure 10-16   Rolling hitch

Sheet Bend

To tie two ropes together, especially those of different thicknesses, use a sheet bend as shown in Figure 10-17.

This completes the basics of sailing. When you feel *totally* confident in your ability to perform all the skills covered so far, and you have correctly answered the questions following

Figure 10-17   Sheet bend

each chapter and section, you will be ready to try a more specialized branch of sailing. This could be racing, boardsailing, or cruising. An introductory chapter to each of these activities follows in part 3.

Checkpoints for Sailing Rules, Care of Your Boat, Rope Work, and Further Knots

1. Are you uneasy about right-of-way situations?

    (a) First determine if you are on the same or different tacks. If the same, windward boat must keep clear; if different, port tack boat must keep clear; if you cannot tell, keep clear if you are on port.

    (b) If you are involved in overtaking, the overtaking boat keeps clear.

2. Are you taking good care of your boat? If you notice a problem arising, such as excessive wear on part of the hull or sail, find out what is causing it and take steps to reduce it. Consider the following examples:

    (a) If the sail is worn by contact with the shrouds, use plastic shroud protectors.

    (b) If the sail seems permanently creased, do not fold along this line when storing.

    (c) If the hull is damaged, has this occurred when the boat was on a trailer? When she was being launched or recovered? Or when she was tied up at the dock?

    (d) Are you storing your spars flat?

    (e) Are you storing your boat at the correct temperature and humidity?

3. Can you heave a line accurately? If not, check to ensure that

    (a) the line is neatly coiled, ready to run out;

    (b) you have divided the line so that one third is in your throwing hand;

    (c) you are throwing underhand in a swinging motion.

    (d) you are overthrowing so that some part of the rope lands on target.

Questions on Chapter 10

1. Give the right-of-way boat in each situation, and say why she held the right-of-way:

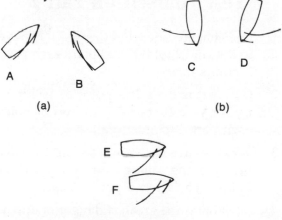

2. Name three specific items you would check for possible repair/replacement at the end of the sailing season.

3. What are some advantages and disadvantages of synthetic rope?

4. (a) What types of rope construction are there?

    (b) Which would you choose for a sheet?

    (c) Why?

5. What are the names for the two distinct sections of a rope?

6. What should you do when heaving a line?

7. For what purpose would you use a sheet bend?

Activities for Chapter 10

1. Make some flat, cardboard, boat-shaped models and color each one differently. Insert a piece of wire to represent the boom. Cut out an arrow shape for the wind. Set up various situations and discuss which boat has the right-of-way, and why.

2. Inspect your boat to see if there is excessive wear anywhere, and take steps to correct this. Check if any parts need replacement and keep a list.

3. Get some old, unusable pieces of rope and cut them into short lengths. Whip the ends; then make a splice and eye splice.

4. Tidy up your sailing area by recoiling all the ropes that look untidy, and hang them appropriately.

5. Practice heaving a line to someone, or make a target. As your skill improves, increase the distance you to have to throw.

6. Tie a round turn and two half hitches, a rolling hitch, and a sheet bend.

Test Yourself on Part 2

1. (a) What is a safe wind direction (relative to the land)? (b) Why? (1 point each part; 2 points total)

2. (a) What is the safest point of sailing to try for your first sail? (b) Why? (1 point each part; 2 points total)

3. What are five factors you should consider before going sailing in a new place? (1 point each factor; 5 points total)

4. (a) What is the greatest danger of downwind sailing? (b) How can you avoid or minimize it? (1 point each part; 2 points total)

5. Give the two commands and the response for coming about and explain exactly when they are spoken. (1 point each; 6 points total)

6. What three tools are needed to whip a rope? (1 point each; 3 points total)

7. In each of the following situations, which boat has the right-of-way? Explain why: (1 point each; 3 points total)

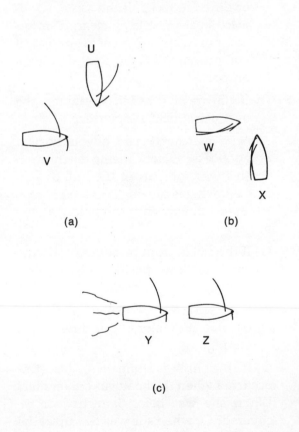

8. Use a dotted line to indicate the path and a sail outline to indicate the point of sailing and tack you are on when following these instructions:

Sail from A to B on a starboard run. Leave B to port and head for C without gybing. Leave C to starboard and reach back to B. Leave B to starboard and plot the most efficient course back to A. Assume constant wind and no current. (1 point for each correct response; 8 points total)

• C

B
•

➡ •

A

9. Your boat is making sternway and you wish to turn the bow to port. To which side do you move the tiller? (1 point total)

Scores:

32-30 Excellent. You were born to sail!

29-25 Good. Just a few points to get clear.

24-20 Fair. Try rereading the chapters.

Below 20 Poor. Do not give up. First, reread the chapters, and then ask your more experienced friends or your instructor if you may sail with them to observe and ask questions. Next, repeat the Activities sections and then retake the test.

Now, go on to those sections of part 3 that seem to be the most fun.

Part 3

Increasing Your Fun

11

Racing: Basic Rules and Strategy

Becoming a good racing helmsperson takes years of practice, but an understanding of the points covered in this chapter will give you a working knowledge of the rules, enabling you to start using some basic tactics.

Objectives

- To understand basic racing rules and principles
- To plan a good start and sail an efficient course
- To know the correct procedure for protesting
- To answer the questions on p. 102

Helpful Terms

Mark. Alternative name for buoy.

To luff another boat. To attempt to prevent a boat from passing you to windward by forcing her to luff up.

"Mast abeam." Called by the windward boat to stop the leeward boat from luffing her; the windward boat's helmsperson must be abeam of the leeward boat's mast.

"Water." Called by a boat claiming room to maneuver at a buoy.

Favored end. The better end of the line from which to start.

Blanketing. Sailing between another boat and the wind.

Windward/weather buoy. The buoy arrived at by beating.

Overstanding. Beating toward a buoy and sailing on too far before tacking.

Layline. Course permitting a beating boat to clear the windward buoy.

Windshadow. Area of reduced wind strength caused by an intervening sail or other obstacle.

Luffing match. Contest between leeward and windward boat in which the leeward tries to prevent the windward from overtaking.

Covertacking. Copying the tacking maneuvers of the boat behind to prevent her from passing you.

Spinnaker. Lightweight and often brightly colored sail set in front of the mast for downwind sailing.

Objectives of Sailboat Racing

In sailing races, visual and audible signals are given at specific time intervals in a countdown to indicate the exact time of the start. Unlike most other types of races where competitors start from a position at rest, in sailing boats move about before the start. The ideal place to be when the starting signal sounds is exactly on the start line, going as fast as possible in the direction of the first buoy. Thereafter you sail around a series of buoys in a predetermined order and direction. Obeying all the rules and committing no infractions, you compete to be the first across the finish line. Paddling, sculling or other nonsailing propulsion is, of course, not allowed.

In the following pages, the basic rules that govern sailboat racing are first explained, followed by a section on strategy to encourage you to make the most of your new sport. Do not be discouraged if you finish in 23rd place; instead, resolve to make it at least 22nd next time!

Preparation for Racing

Organizing an unofficial race among beginning sailors like yourself or holding a race in class make for ideal learning situations because they can be kept short and informal. The first time around the course, you might all agree just to keep out of everyone else's way, but this will soon become unsatisfactory because no clear rights-of-way have been established. You will want to learn the basic rules and continue building on your understanding of them.

Another excellent preparation to gain understanding of the rules in action before you take the helm is to crew for an experienced racing helmsperson.

If you are not in a class situation and if you do not know any racing helmsperson, you might decide to enter some organized races. Just keep out of everyone else's way until your confidence and knowledge grow.

Equipment Needed

Buy a copy of the complete sailing rule book by writing to your national sailing authority (see Appendix C for a list of addresses) as you will often need to refer to the rules. Sailboat racing has over 70 rules, and anyone intending to race regularly must gradually become familiar with each one; however, you can take part in your first race when you know just a few. Not to know even these rules would put you at a disadvantage and could spoil your own enjoyment, or worse, someone else's.

An accurate, waterproof stopwatch is an essential piece of equipment for anyone in any type of race.

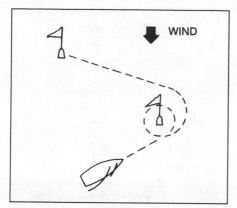

Figure 11-1 Rerounding a buoy after hitting it

Basic Racing Rules

The racing rules come into effect at your preparatory or warning signal, which is usually given 5 minutes before the start. Before that time, keep clear of others because you are governed by the Rules of the Road (see chapter 10).

Contact With Other Boats

A concept you must grasp is that neither you nor your boat may touch any other boat or a buoy of the course. Because no umpire watches each boat's every move, all sailors are on their honor to abide by the rules. If you do touch another boat and she held the right-of-way, you must either (a) retire from the race; (b) sail your boat around in a circle twice doing a 720° turn, which gives you a time penalty, and then continue the race; or (c) accept a penalized finishing position. The race committee should inform you which procedure they are using. In informal races, you can usually resolve a problem on the water by agreeing to sail on and then discuss it afterwards. Once you start organized races, however, you must follow an established procedure for resolving disputes (see the Protest Procedure section in this chapter).

Contact With a Mark/Buoy

If you hit a *mark*, or buoy, of the course, you must complete the rounding and then reround it to make a loop around it (see Figure 11-1).

While rerounding, you must keep clear of everyone else.

Rights of Way

Knowing which boat has right-of-way and which must keep clear is crucial in sailing races. The following are the basic rules covering many situations you may encounter when beginning to race.

Boats on opposite tacks. When boats on opposite tacks meet, the port tack boat must give way to the starboard tack boat. Remember, a port tack boat has the wind blowing over the port side and the sail on the starboard side. If you are the port tack boat, *how* you keep out of the way is up to you. You may either come about, or sail behind the stern of the other boat; or if you are absolutely certain that you can cross ahead of the other boat without her having to alter course, then you may hold your course. This, however, requires nerve and should not be used unless you are absolutely certain you can make it in front of the other boat.

Sometimes when boats converge, it is not immediately obvious that you are on opposite tacks, as in these diagrams, but the same factors apply as in the more obvious opposite tack situations (see Figure 11-2).

Boats on the same tack. When boats are on the same tack and converging, the one to windward of the other must keep clear. The windward one is the one nearer to the direction from which the wind is coming. Again, there are several examples of this occurrence, some more obvious than others (see Figure 11-3).

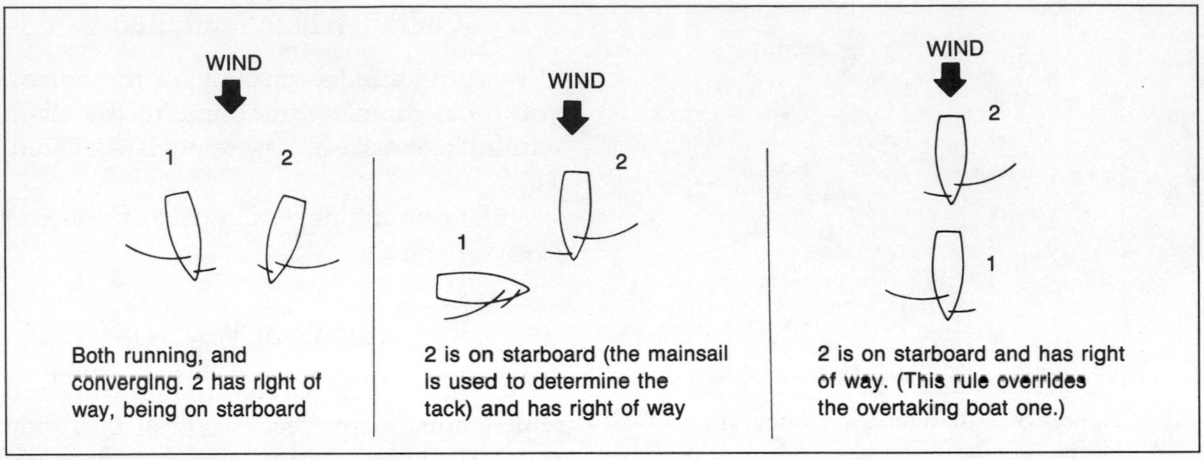

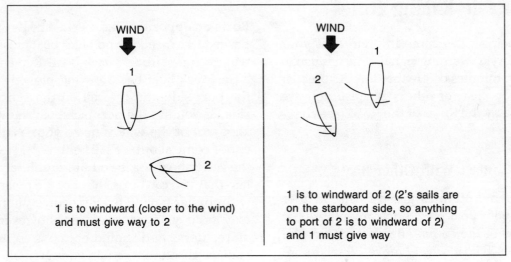

Figure 11-2 Opposite tack situations

Figure 11-3 Windward/leeward situations

Boats overtaking.   When one boat overtakes another, the overtaking boat must keep clear of the one being overtaken. If you are the overtaking boat, you have a choice: to keep out of the way to windward or to leeward (see Figure 11-4).

If you go to windward, you have the advantage of keeping the wind from the sails of the other boat, but because you thereby become the windward boat, you must keep clear of the leeward boat. She is allowed to force you head to wind, or *luff* you, in an attempt

to stop you overtaking. You must avoid hitting her. She can continue to luff to protect her position until you are in a *mast abeam* position. This means your helmsperson is level with her mast (see Figure 11-5).

Then shout, "Mast abeam," and she must immediately return to her normal course to the next buoy.

You may choose to overtake to leeward of the other boat. She is thus the windward boat and may not fall off toward you. This is undoubtedly the safer side for overtaking until

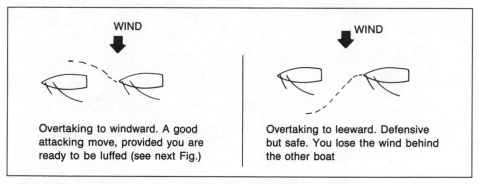

Figure 11-4   Two methods for the overtaking boat to keep clear

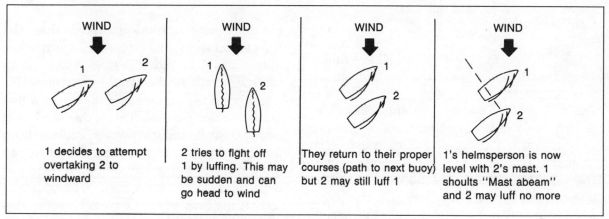

Figure 11-5   Stopping a boat luffing by achieving "mast abeam"

you become more sure of the rules; however, it is the disadvantageous side because you lose the wind behind the other boat.

Boats at buoys.   At a buoy, the boat that gets there first, rounds it first, and the others keep clear. Complications arise if boats overlap one another (see Figure 11-6).

When B shouts, "*Water,* please," A must give B room to round the buoy, unless it is a starting marker, as long as B established her overlap on A more than two boat's lengths before the buoy. This means you cannot charge up to a buoy in the last seconds before rounding and expect to be given room. If you did not get an overlap before the two boat's lengths distance, you should round the buoy outside all the other boats. Often many

boats arrive at a buoy together as in Figure 11-7.

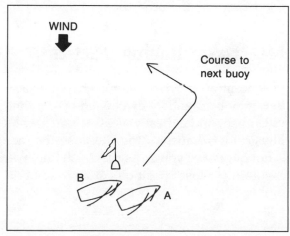

Figure 11-6   Giving room at a buoy

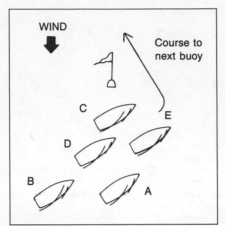

Figure 11-7 Giving and not giving room at a buoy

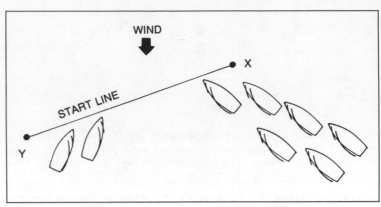

Figure 11-8 Favored end of the start line

Here, A has to give room to all the other boats except B.

Boats changing course. Another basic rule to know relates to changing tacks or gybing. A boat that is tacking or gybing must keep clear of a boat on a tack. This prevents you from making a maneuver too close to someone else. If you want to tack or gybe in a large fleet, your only remedy might be to lose speed (e.g., by spilling wind from the sail) and then to drop back clear of the other boats. To avoid these problems, do not come about in front of another boat unless you know you can establish right-of-way on your new course in good time for the other boat to avoid you.

Basic Racing Tactics

Concentrate hard every moment of the race. You may be mentally exhausted by the time you finish, and in heavy weather you may be physically exhausted, too. Because the race is not over until you cross the finish line, you can gain (or lose) positions at any moment.

Tactics at the Start

Usually, start at the favored end of the line. Get to the starting area in good time if you can do so without hindering boats that start before you and make a few trial approaches to the line. Although race committees try to set lines at 90° to the wind, sometimes this is not possible. Many races start from a line that has a *favored* end. This is the windward end of the line, and it is favored because from this end, you can steer a course that takes you more directly to the first buoy. To find out which end of a line is favored, make your boat luff on the line. If your bow is closer to one end of the line, that is the windward end. In Figure 11-8, X is the windward or favored end of the line, and this advantage is compounded by the fact that boats starting at the X end are on starboard tack.

Occasionally, start at the nonfavored end of the line. Most boats would start at the X end in Figure 11-8, so occasionally you may be able to make quite a good start at the Y end where there are fewer boats. If the nonfavored end is much worse, this would not be a good tactic, however alone you were.

Start with clear wind. Strive to start with clear wind in your sails and not be to leeward of another boat's sail or you will be *blanketed*. In Figure 11-9, A has the clear wind and thus the best start. To get clear wind, make for an uncrowded section of the line.

Time your approach to the line. Having decided where on the line you plan to start, and on which tack, the next thing to decide

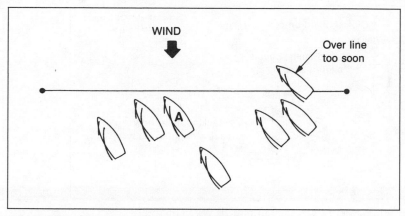

WIND

Over line
too soon

A

Figure 11-9 Good, nonblanketed position

is how you will approach that spot and how you will time your approach. Usually, you can use sightings from landmarks to pinpoint a position from which to start the timed approach. Do this several times to determine an average time. It is best to arrive in the vicinity of the starting line a fraction early because you can always slow the boat down by spilling wind, but you cannot speed her up. Having found, for example, that it takes you 23 seconds to get from your landmark to the line, arrive at your spot about 20 seconds before the start and head for the line. Aim to have the boat going at full speed at the start signal, even if you have spilled wind on your approach to the start.

Do not cross the line before the starting signal because if you do, you will be recalled and will have to restart. You will have to turn back and recross the line, wasting valuable time. You must also keep out of every other boat's way while doing this, even if you are on starboard tack and they are on port. Clearly, it does not pay to be over the line too soon; on the other hand, if you are not over it occasionally, you are probably starting too late.

Tactics During the Race

Once the race has started, you can employ many techniques to help you gain places or to maintain the lead.

Always be alert for windshifts, and watch to see if other boats alter course, too. If they seem to be going better on the other tack, do not get left behind—you also come about. Failure to notice and to take advantage of even small windshifts is a most significant factor in determining your finishing position. Some windshifts last, some do not. If a shift continues for more than about 5 seconds, assume it will stay. Tack every time a lasting shift forces you to head more away from the buoy than you were heading. As the course on one tack worsens, so it improves on the other (see Figure 11-10).

A few well-judged, long tacks are usually better than many short tacks because you lose speed every time you come about. The first tacks should be long; then shorten them as you approach the buoy, if necessary.

Accurately judge your final approach to the mark you must beat up to (the *windward mark*). Because everyone will be converging on this point, you should plan to approach it on starboard tack, thus having the right-of-way over those on port tack.

Do not waste time by sailing beyond the straight-line course on the other tack to the buoy, called *overstanding* (see Figure 11-11).

Here, B has already sailed on beyond her *layline* (the course to the buoy without tacking) and is wasting time. A's plotted course is ideal.

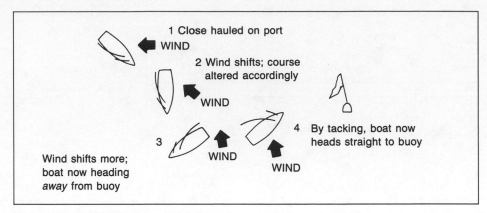

Figure 11-10   Tacking in windshifts

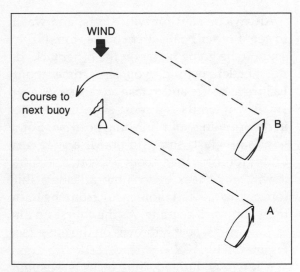

Figure 11-11   Wasting time by overstanding

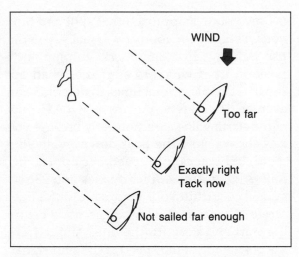

Figure 11-12   Judging when to come about to get to a buoy exactly

Because your new course will be at about 90° to your old course, come about when you reach the point from which you can beat directly to the buoy (see Figure 11-12), but allow for leeway.

If you are racing in tidal waters, some courses that seem poor may turn out to be winners because they pass through tidal currents that are helpful. Find out as much as possible about tides; listen to what people will tell you and do some investigating on your own, too. Spend a day out on the ocean with paper and pencil noting down exactly what the current does at certain key places every hour of the tide.

Watch the courses other boats sail to ensure that if you are going to cross another boat's course, you cross with your boat having right-of-way.

Avoid tacking in someone else's *windshadow*, which is the area of interrupted airflow behind a sail. Foresee where you will be in 20 seconds time, and tack early if you would give yourself a disadvantage by hanging on. Equally, hold off tacking awhile if that will help you.

If, in Figure 11-13, A tacks now, she will have to sail through B's windshadow. If A remains on starboard a few seconds, she can then tack to windward of B.

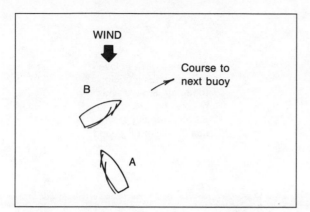

Figure 11-13 Judging when to come about by thinking ahead

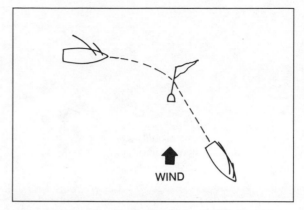

Figure 11-15 Approach the buoy wide so as to depart close

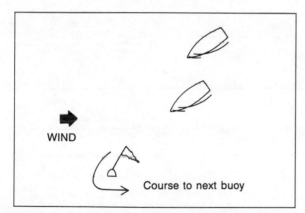

Figure 11-14 Keeping to leeward for the inside berth

Tactics at Buoys

Try to get inside position when approaching the buoy so that others will have to give you room, but remember that you must establish your overlap at least two boat's lengths before the buoy to be able to claim room. Sometimes you can encourage a boat to try to pass you to windward if that would give you inside position (see Figure 11-14).

When you round a buoy from a reach and head up to sail close-hauled, approach the buoy wide and depart close, as in Figure 11-15.

Sailing a good course to the next buoy is much more important than the last few yards of the leg you are just finishing. A few degrees angle of difference in course heading at the start of a leg makes a vast difference at the end of the leg, and you want to ensure that no other boat gets upwind of you (see Figure 11-16).

Tactics for Protecting Your Position

Avoid being blanketed by sailing off to one side or the other of a rival boat and getting clear wind. Once this is achieved, head back on course. Try not to get involved in lengthy one-on-one battles (*luffing matches*) where the leeward boat heads up to try to prevent an overtaking boat coming past to windward because this takes you off course. Sometimes, while you are fighting one boat, the rest of the fleet sails past, and although you may have prevented one boat from overtaking, that does not mean much if all the others have passed you (see Figure 11-17).

Of course, if you are leading approaching the finish and another boat is catching up, by all means luff to protect your position. Do likewise if you are approaching a buoy but never get involved in head-to-head competition that leaves you in a worse position than before.

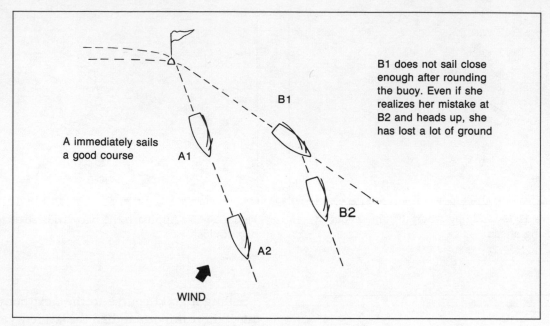

Figure 11-16 Immediately after rounding, set a good course

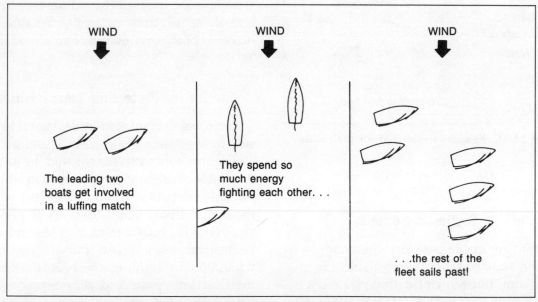

Figure 11-17 Involvement in a luffing match may lose many places

Tactics for Improving Your Finishing Position

Even if after much practice you still consistently finish well down the fleet, it may be worthwhile sitting out an entire race to watch what the leaders do. If you still finish toward the back of the fleet, try copying the leaders. Alternatively, offer to crew for winning helmspeople. Just observe and listen, and you will learn many new tactics that you may later use against the same people.

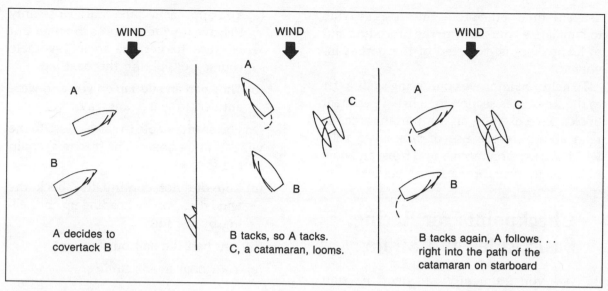

Figure 11-18   Covertacking bluff

Tactics When Leading

One glorious day after many hours of practice, you will find yourself in the lead. Now you can adopt the plan of duplicating what the second boat does (*covertacking*) so she cannot pass you. Be aware of the third boat, but have your crew closely watch the second boat. Every time she tacks, you tack. In this way, if she happens to find a favorable windshift, you do too. Of course, if she makes a poor move, so do you. However, be aware. The second boat may deliberately pull a covertack bluff maneuver so that you will copy her and end up in a worse position than before (see Figure 11-18).

Protest Procedure

When you enter organized races, you need to be aware of your rights and responsibilities. If (a) you see two boats make contact, (b) you see a boat infringing a rule and not making amends, or (c) a boat hits you and you think she was in the wrong, you may file a protest. Because this is a part of everyday racing procedure, it should never be considered unsporting to protest unless your reason is frivolous. The intent of the rules is to promote fair sailing and to reduce the number and seriousness of collisions, but do not insist on your right-of-way on every occasion. Always alter course, even if you are sure you are right, to avoid serious damage.

If you feel you have a case for protesting against another boat, first inform that boat immediately of your intentions. This gives her crew a chance to absolve themselves if they consider they were in the wrong. Next, fly the red swallow-tailed protest flag, which is International Code Flag B. [In the U.K. a white handkerchief is an acceptable substitute.]

After the race, complete a protest form stating the facts of the incident and the rule(s) you consider infringed. The club forms a committee to hear the protest; then you and your opponent give evidence. Both may call witnesses. The committee deliberates and makes its decision, often disqualifying a boat. The committee's purpose is to ensure that the rules are observed and if you think you have observed them, give the committee a chance to prove you were right. If you are daunted by the idea of protest meetings, ask if you may listen to some of the protest meetings at a club to familiarize yourself with the procedure and to learn what is expected of the parties involved.

To help you improve your racing skills, refer to the Resources section for a list of pertinent books. Two exciting and important areas to read about are the use of *spinnaker* sails, which are used on reaches and runs, and how to tune your boat for maximum performance.

Checkpoints for Racing: Basic Rules and Strategy

1. Are you frequently late over the start line? Did you

    (a) get out on the water in good time?

    (b) time several practice starts?

    (c) start 5 seconds early? You may find yourself at the line right on time, even though you thought you would be early.

2. Were you unsure of where to start? Did you

    (a) check by luffing to see which end was the favored end?

    (b) think about starting on port tack, if this would give you clear wind?

3. Did you have difficulty approaching the windward mark? Did you consider

    (a) any tides or currents and figure in their effect?

    (b) the windshadow effect from any obstacles?

    (c) finding the layline by sighting abeam of your boat and figuring in leeway?

    (d) arriving on starboard tack?

    (e) windshifts?

4. Did you let other boats cut in at marks? The reason(s) could be the following:

    (a) You approached the mark close only to leave it wide. Approach wider but be sure to get the most favorable course possible on the next leg.

    (b) They had an overlap on you and were entitled to water anyway.

5. Do you seem unable to sail as close to the wind as other boats? The reason(s) could be the following:

    (a) You did not continually check the wind direction by heading up and sailing by the luff.

    (b) You had the sail out too far.

    (c) Your boat needs tuning.

Questions on Chapter 11

1. If a forceful collision seems imminent, but you are certain that you have the right-of-way, what should you do?

2. When do racing rules come into operation?

3. In each of the diagrams below, indicate which boat has the right of way and explain why. Assume that the boats are racing.

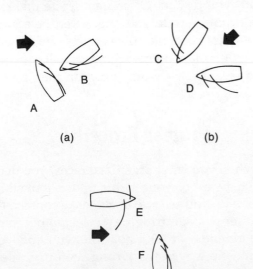

(a)   (b)

(c)

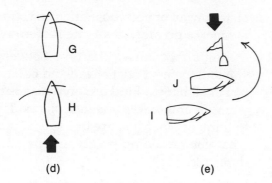

(d)   (e)

4. (a) In a race, if you feel you were in the right and another boat was in the wrong, but the other boat will not acknowledge wrongdoing, what can you do?

    (b) How?

5. (a) Which is the favored end of this starting line?

    (b) Why?

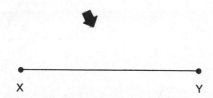

6. (a) If the wind changes from Situation 1 to 2, does it make getting to the buoy easier or more difficult?

    (b) What should you adjust on the boat?

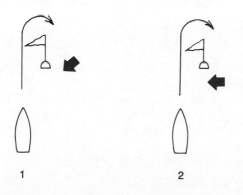

1   2

7. Draw the layline for this boat. The buoy is to be left to starboard.

8. Draw the course you would take around this buoy so that your course to the next buoy was as favorable as possible.

9. (a) What is meant by covertacking?
    (b) When would you use it?
    (c) When would you not use it?

Activities for Chapter 11

1. Make the boat and wind models explained on p. 86. In addition, make some circles to represent buoys. Use these models to discuss points that arose during your races.

2. Set up a start line and a windward mark. Take it in turns to act as starter and practice starting. The winner is the first to round the buoy.

3. Set up a fair, or nonfavored, start line. Start boats in pairs from either end of the line and have beating duels to the windward mark. Make sure the rules are observed.

4. Sit out a race and observe. Write down on an outline map where the leading three boats crossed the line. Draw their paths to the first buoy and even if they lose ground to others, continue to follow these three. Try to account for their maneuvers.

5. Volunteer to crew for several different people. Learn what works for them and what does not and why. Do ask questions, but *not* when the helmsperson is busy planning and carrying out strategy!

6. Practice rounding buoys by both coming about and gybing until you have complete control of your boat and can round the marks no more than one foot away.

7. During a race, check the time between you and the next boat ahead and behind you at all buoys. Find out on which legs you gain and where you lose places. Try to think of what you are doing well and what you are doing poorly and practice the latter.

8. Hold a protest meeting in your class. You will need a chairperson and some committee members to determine the outcome and a helmsperson and crew for each side. Take turns at the different positions. If an incident arises during one of your races in class, have a protest meeting afterwards.

9. Practice turning your boat through 720° as quickly as possible.

12

Introduction to Boardsailing

Once you have mastered the basics of sailing, you may be attracted to boardsailing. Although you will be helped by the similarity of the theory to dinghy sailing, the techniques of maneuvering are very different.

Objectives

- To know the basic terminology of sailboards
- To understand how a sailboard differs from a dinghy
- To sail a sailboard on all points of sailing
- To come about and gybe a sailboard
- To answer the questions on p. 114

Helpful Terms

Skeg. Fin at the stern.

Uphaul. Rope used to pull a sail up out of the water.

Mast hand. The hand nearer the mast.

Sheet hand. The hand nearer the stern, acting as a sheet.

Rake. To incline the mast forward/backward and/or side/side.

Once you understand the principles of small boat sailing, you may think of trying other branches of the sport, such as boardsailing. Boardsailing is the same thing as windsurfing, but a Windsurfer is one particular brand of sailboard. The fundamentals of boardsailing, which you can more easily understand now that you know the basics of sailing, are covered in this chapter.

Read the entire chapter before trying boardsailing; then try each of these maneuvers in the order of presentation.

Equipment

In all but the warmest weather a wet suit is essential because you will be spending much time in the water while you learn! Wet suit bootees give a good grip, provided they have a ribbed sole and are not merely neoprene socks. If you feel the need for gloves, inexpensive household rubber gloves give a good grip.

Boardsailors stand divided on the life jacket question. Some feel that wearing one could create a dangerous situation if the mast falls on you, and you are not able to go beneath the water to avoid it. Others believe that a compact life jacket does provide buoyancy for all the time spent in the water, and that if by chance you get separated from your board, a life jacket could be a lifesaver. You are urged to wear one and to get into the habit of putting up your hands, with the palms flat to prevent breaking a finger, to protect yourself from the falling mast.

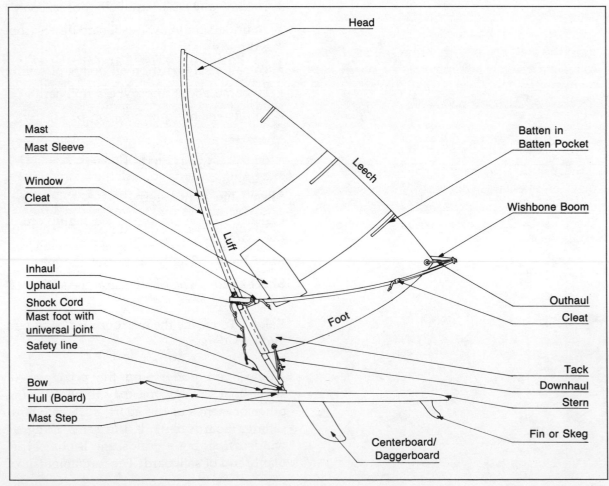

Figure 12-1 Parts of a sailboard

Parts of a Sailboard

The major difference between a sailboard and a regular sailboat is that the former has no rudder and is steered by mast rake and weight distribution adjustments. Many of the parts of the boat are the same, but the most important parts are shown in Figure 12-1.

Use a Simulator

If you have access to a sailboard simulator, use it for the following drill. If you do not, a comparable alternative can be made by rigging the sail of a sailboard and by sticking the foot of the mast in the sand or ground, or by actually stepping the mast into a sailboard from which the daggerboard and any fins at the stern (*skegs*) have been removed. For rigging the sail, see p. 108. From the start, try to realize that it is holding onto the boom and leaning into the wind that provide your greatest sources of stability.

Raise the Sail

Start with your back to the wind and the mast joint between your feet. With your knees bent, grasp the line connected to the boom at the forward end, called the *uphaul*, in both hands. Pull along it hand over hand, straightening your knees, so that you gradually raise up the sail. Continue until you have hold of the end of the boom with both hands. The sail will now be streaming away from you (see Figure 12-2). This is the starting position.

This starting position is where you will start every time you pull the sail up out of the water; it is akin to the luffing position in a dinghy. From here you could sail off on either tack. For the sake of example, we will have you sail here on a starboard tack—sailing so that your right shoulder will be leading. Thus your right hand will be called the *mast hand* (the hand nearer the mast), and your left hand will be called the *sheet hand* (the hand further from the mast and the one acting exactly as a sheet because it pulls in or lets out the sail) (see Figure 12-3).

Position Yourself and the Sail

From the position of both hands by the uphaul, cross your right hand over your left to grasp the boom close to the mast. Rake the mast slightly forward and grasp the boom with the left (sheet) hand about 3 feet aft of the right (mast) hand. Pull the boom forward and to windward until the sail begins to fill and you will be off. If ever you feel the sail is taking off with you holding it, do what you would do in a regular sailboat to lose power—

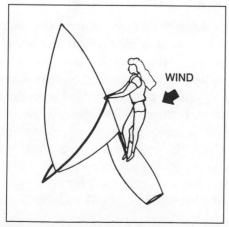

Figure 12-2 Starting position

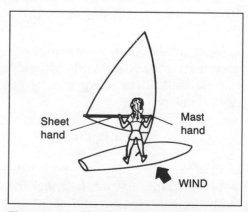

Figure 12-3 Sheet hand/mast hand

ease the sheet out—which in this case means moving your sheet hand slightly closer to the mast hand.

Always keep the mast perpendicular to the ground but practice letting the sail out until it luffs and then sheet it in again. This should be done for both tacks so that each hand has a turn at being the sheet hand and the mast hand, and you are quite clear which hand has which job. Remember:

Front hand—Firm
Rear hand—Releases

Steering

Steering a sailboard is performed by *raking*, or leaning, the mast. Rake it forward and you bear away; rake it backward and you head up. Just as you change your heading or point of sailing, the sail setting must be adjusted, too, by means of the sheet hand.

Play around with your land-based sail to get the feel of adjusting the mast rake to change your heading, and then alter the amount the sail is sheeted in or out to match your heading.

Preparation for Boardsailing

Your first attempts at boardsailing should be on small, confined stretches of water. The water conditions should be flat because you are likely to find balancing to be the most difficult aspect of the sport to master in the early stages. In addition, have someone keep an eye out for you, or sail with a friend, and never boardsail when there is an offshore wind blowing.

Launching

The first step is to maintain your balance. Put your board in the water (without the sail but with the centerboard and skeg) and be

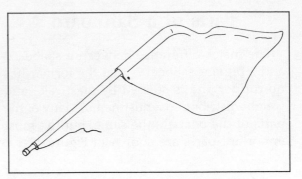

Figure 12-4 Putting the sail on the mast

careful not to step on it until you are in water deeper than any fins protrude. Kneel on the board and paddle out a few yards. Lower the centerboard. Try standing up and kneeling down again several times, always keeping your weight in the middle of the board. It is normal to feel unstable at this point, but when you start sailing, you will have a boom to hold on to and the power of the wind in the sail to hold you up. Now stand up and turn around on the board a few times. Next, jump off and climb back once or twice.

The next step is to fit your sail to the board. When rigging the sail, carry out the following procedure:

1. Slide the mast up inside the sleeve of the mainsail and cleat the downhaul (see Figure 12-4).

2. Position the boom around the sail so it will be at shoulder height and attach the boom to the mast. The knot is shown in Figure 12-5 and should be tied while the boom is up almost parallel with the mast so that when the boom is lowered, the knot is pulled even tighter. You could use a rolling hitch or a clove hitch with a figure eight on the end by the knot. Use whichever works best for your rig to ensure a tight fit of the boom to the mast.

3. Pull the clew outhaul tight and cleat it.

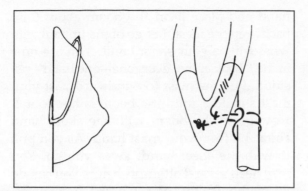

Figure 12-5   Attaching the boom to the mast

Figure 12-6   Carrying the rigged sail

4. Insert any battens.

5. Attach the uphaul, leading it up from below the boom and tying a figure eight knot above. Tie three or four simple overhand knots in the uphaul to give you a better grip.

6. Attach the shock cord from the foot of the mast to the second knot up (refer back to Figure 12-1). This cord keeps the uphaul within reach.

7. Carry the sail to the board as in Figure 12-6.

8. Insert the boom into the mast step and fix it. The easiest way to do this is to place the sail on the water to leeward of the board and turn the board on its side toward the sail. Two of the several different types of mast foot joint are shown in Figure 12-7.

9. Fix the safety line to the board so that if the mast comes out, it cannot get separated from the board (see Figure 12-8).

10. If you are sailing on a large expanse of water, attach a light line of about 150 feet to the skeg, and either tie the other end to a point on shore or have a friend hold it. If you get stuck offshore and are unable to return, you can either pull yourself in or be pulled back to shore.

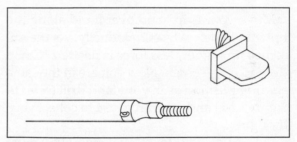

Figure 12-7   Types of mast foot joints

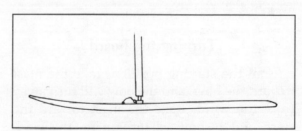

Figure 12-8   Fixing the safety line to the board

Raising the Sail

Insert the centerboard and paddle out to a depth where you can lower it fully. Find the wind direction and position the board at right angles to it with the sail over to leeward.

Climb aboard and grasp the uphaul in both hands and position your feet on each side of the mast as you face the sail. Bend your knees and lean back using your leg muscles as well as your arms to pull the sail up (see Figure 12-9).

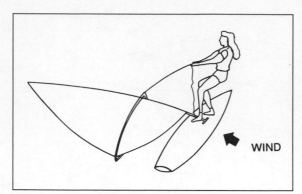

Figure 12-9   Pulling up the sail

Move your grip hand over hand along the uphaul. Pull slowly and gradually. As the sail comes up higher, less force is needed. Grasp the end of the boom. Now you are in the same starting position as in your land drill (refer to Figure 12-2) and you can pause to collect your thoughts.

Before you start to sail, however, you must master one more skill: how to turn the board so you will return.

Turning the Board

From the starting position, rake the mast toward the bow, and the bow will turn away from the wind. Rake the mast toward the stern, and the bow will turn up into the wind. Magic! Decide which way you want to turn the board and make it go around 180° while you take small steps to keep your back to the wind. All the time the board is turning, continue to keep the sail luffing. Turn the board around beneath you several times in both directions until you are completely happy about doing this.

Sailing on Reaches

Now you are ready to try sailing. First, get into the starting position. Then, to start sailing, cross over the hand that will be the mast hand and place it on the boom about 6 in. back from the mast. Let go of the uphaul with what will be your sheet hand. You are now in the "Look at me, everyone—one hand" position. Pull the mast to windward past your mast shoulder until the boom is horizontal. Now grasp the boom with the sheet hand about 3 ft from your mast hand. As you pull in with the sheet hand, away you go. You may need several attempts before you can do this without falling off the board. Remembering to use the sail as your source of stability will make balancing on the board much easier.

If you want to slow down, ease the sail out with the sheet hand. Sound familiar? It is exactly the same principle as easing the sheet in a dinghy. If you need to stop quickly, drop the sail and jump in, but hold on to the board immediately to stop it from floating away.

Steering

As soon as you do manage to keep your balance and begin to sail, you need to try steering. Rake the mast forward and you will bear away; rake it backward and you will head up. For now get on to a reaching point of sail (as in beginning dinghy sailing). This will allow you to return to your starting point easily.

When you have sailed a short distance of no more than about 20 yards, turn the board around and sail back. Continue with these reaches and turns until you are more confident and ready for the next challenge.

Coming About

Although you do already know a way to get the board turned around, there is a much more efficient way. Using this method does not require you to stop, luff, and rotate the board; you actually sail the board around (see Figure 12-10).

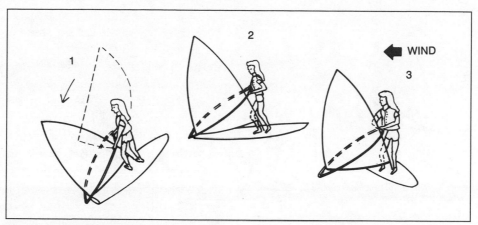

Figure 12-10   Coming about

1. Rake the mast aft and, at the same time, sheet in with the rear or sheet hand. Put most of your weight on your back foot to help the bow turn toward the wind. Continue to rake the mast aft until the sail begins to luff.

2. Keeping the sail raked back, begin to walk around the front of the mast. You should use small steps. First, cross your sheet hand over to grasp the boom handle or uphaul; also grasp this handle/uphaul with the front hand. As you walk around the front of the mast, keep the rig raked back.

3. Continue to turn the board by keeping the rig raked back and by walking the board around so that you are back in your starting position, but on the other tack, with the board at 90° to the wind and the sail streaming out to leeward. By all means, pause at this point to collect your thoughts. When you are ready to go again, grasp the boom near the mast with the new mast hand and rake the sail to windward until the boom is horizontal; then sheet in with the new rear sheet hand to catch the wind. Lean backward with a straight back to counter the wind.

Gybing

Gybing a sailboard is a somewhat different concept from gybing a regular sailboat, because in the former, the sail goes around the front of the boat. Refer to Figure 12-11 and then follow these steps:

1. From a reach, head the boat more downwind by raking the rig more toward the front of the board. Ease out with the sheet hand. Rake the whole rig more across to the mast side and have one foot on either side of the board and face forward. You should now be looking where you are going through the window in the sail. This is running.

2. Release the boom from the sheet hand and grasp the boom handle or boom end of the uphaul in your sheet hand. Grasp the uphaul with your mast hand, too. Lean the mast more to the old sheet side and use your weight to turn the board more. The sail will go around by the bow and you will be back in the starting position.

3. Cross over the new mast hand, and grasp the boom with the new mast hand and then the new sheet hand. Sheet in.

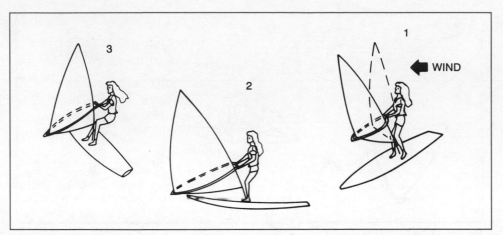

Figure 12-11 Gybing

Getting the Sail
Back to the Leeward Side

When you fall off in the early stages and then climb back on, you invariably find that the rig is the "wrong way" around: The sail has fallen in the water to windward. To correct this, get up on the board, grasp the up-haul, and pull up until there is just a little wind getting under the sail. Now you can use the wind to swing the sail over to the leeward side while you quickly walk around the mast with small steps to balance the board. Once you have your back to the wind and the sail on the leeward side, you are back in your regular starting position.

Beating

As with dinghy sailing, you have started off by reaching, but as soon as possible you should work on upwind sailing. Again, there is a real temptation to run downwind but then find yourself unable to beat back. To change direction from a reach to a beat, rake the rig back, but keep it upright and sheet in hard. Put your weight on your back foot to push the board into heading up. As soon as you are on a beating course, return the rig to a slightly forward position so that you sail straight.

When beating, the mast is held close to the body, and the end of the boom should be over the leeward aft corner of the board. If the sail flaps, bear away by raking the mast forward. Remember to sheet well in with the sheet hand.

Running

To change direction from a reach to a run, rake the rig forward and put your weight on your front foot to force the bow away from the wind. Ease out with the sheet hand. Turn to face forward (you should be looking through the window in the sail now) with one foot slightly ahead of the other for stability. Once you have got on to a run, return the rig to a more upright position.

Self-Rescue Techniques

If you do get stranded, you need to be aware of a couple of self-rescue techniques.

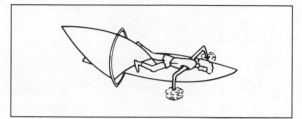

Figure 12-12 Self-rescue position

If you have a relatively short way to paddle back, place the rig on top of the board so that the sail is out of the water, as in Figure 12-12. You can then either kneel on, sit astride, or lie along the board and paddle back, using either your hands or the centerboard. If you have a long way to return, undo the clew outhaul. Next, remove the mast from the board, having made sure the safety line is attached, and fold the boom up to the mast. Remove the battens and push them up inside the mast sleeve, roll the sail up to the mast/boom as tightly as possible, and place along the center of the board. Again, sit, kneel, or lie on the board and paddle back.

Transporting a Sailboard

Transporting a board on a car roof is easy. Place it bow first and upside down for the best aerodynamics. If you place it on right way up, the board may take off when the car is going at speed.

Once you have grasped these elementary aspects of board sailing, you can go on to racing or to funboard or freestyle sailing. The Resources section contains information on these skills.

Checkpoints for Boardsailing

1. Did you have trouble balancing on the board? The problem(s) could be

    (a) not having your weight amidships;

    (b) not using the power of the wind in the sail to balance against;

    (c) insufficient practice! Balancing is difficult, and it is not surprising if you take a while. Most people do. Practice balancing with just the board and no sail.

2. Did you have trouble getting going on a reach? You must

    (a) check to ensure that your board is at right angles to the wind before raising the sail;

    (b) pull the mast well over to windward with your mast hand so the boom is horizontal before you sheet in;

    (c) keep the right-angles-to-the-wind position as you sheet in.

3. Did you have trouble coming about? Remember to

    (a) sheet in hard;

    (b) rake the mast back;

    (c) keep the mast back while you walk around;

    (d) keep the mast over on the side on which you were standing until the board is around far enough.

4. Did you have trouble beating successfully? The problem(s) could be the following:

    (a) Not getting on course—first alter course to a beat by raking the mast backward, then sheet in hard and get the mast back to its normal position;

    (b) Trying to sail too close to the wind—just as in small boat sailing, you need an angle of 45° to the wind before you can make progress;

    (c) Not sheeting in really hard.

Questions on Chapter 12

1. Name these parts of a sailboard:

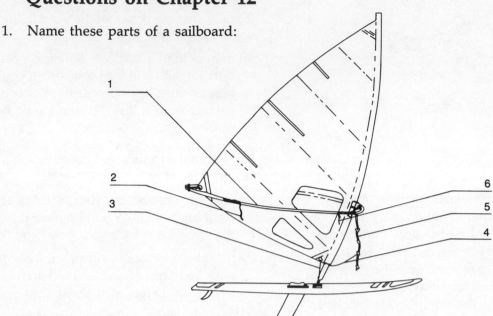

2. What is the starting position in which you want to have the board and sail?

3. Which way do you rake the rig to head up and/or come about?

4. If you fall in with the sail to windward, what is an easy way to return to the starting position?

5. Give two ways you can position the sail to effect a self-rescue.

Activities for Chapter 12

1. Set out two buoys about 50 yards apart so that a line between them is at right angles to the wind. Reach from one buoy to the other, head up, and come about around it. (Refer back to Figure 6-4.) Repeat several times. Be sure that the buoy you are going around will neither be damaged by nor damage your sail if the sail falls on top of it.

2. Set out two buoys as in Figure 6-4, reach between them, then fall off and gybe around them. Repeat several times.

3. Set out a series of buoys in line with the wind about 20 yards apart. Start at the upwind end and "slalom" through between the buoys on broad reaches, gybing as you zigzag.

4. Have your friend ashore blow a whistle (once to come about, twice to gybe).

5. Practice sailing and then letting the sail flap with you holding on with only the mast hand. Get going again. Repeat.

13

Crewing in Larger Boats

Small boats provide good training for larger boat sailing. The principles are similar but on a larger scale, and the complexities are greater. In this chapter you'll get an idea of what to expect.

Objectives

- To know the basic terminology for a cruiser
- To be a useful crew on an offshore cruiser
- To answer the questions on p. 121

Helpful Terms

Tender. Small boat used to ferry the crew to an anchored boat.

Pump the bilges. To remove water from the bottom of the boat.

Gaskets. Sail ties.

Fender. Cushioning device placed between the hull and another object to prevent damage to hull.

Weigh anchor. To pull up the anchor.

Cringle. Metal grommeted hole in sail.

Skirt the jib. To manually adjust the foot of the jib so that it takes a more efficient shape.

Topping lift. Rope or wire attached to the outer end of the boom to take the boom's weight.

Riding turn. A turn around a winch that rides up over the others and jams them.

Tailing a winch. Putting the rope around the winch and collecting it off the winch while someone else winds.

Setting up the backstays. Tensioning and releasing the backstays as the boat comes about or gybes.

Preventer. Additional rope rigged to prevent movement, often on the boom to prevent an accidental gybe.

Preparing to Crew

When you have sailed in small boats for a while, you may want to try sailing on larger cruiser boats. Cruisers usually have fixed keels, so there is no centerboard to adjust, and they generally have sleeping accommodations. Small boat sailing is, however, an ideal training for this size of boat because the principles are the same.

Most people first sail on a larger boat because they are invited by friends or family. For this reason, what follows will be a guide to how to be useful on board a larger boat, rather than directions on how to skipper such a boat. You would be *most* unwise to take charge of a large boat without previous crewing experience.

Reading through this chapter prior to your first experience on a cruiser will help you understand some new ideas not previously encountered while small boat sailing. Cruising is essentially a team effort and the more you can help, the more welcome you will be.

Parts of a Cruiser

The major difference between a dinghy and a cruiser is, of course, size. A wheel may replace a tiller, and there will be many new pieces of equipment unfamiliar to you. A diagram of a typical cruiser and her most important parts are shown in Figure 13-1.

Equipment Needed

Make sure you take enough warm clothing and waterproofs. Open water is much rougher and cooler than sheltered inland areas. Nonslip deck shoes are essential and need not be expensive. Canvas uppers are fine as long as the grip is good. Also bring food and drink for you are likely to be out for several hours.

Getting Under Way

When you arrive at the boat, apart from the obvious size increase, the first difference you'll notice is that a large boat is kept afloat either on a mooring, at anchor, or berthed in a marina. If you approach your boat via a small boat, or *tender*, which is used to ferry you to the large boat, be careful not to get your fingers trapped between the two boats. For this reason, never hold a boat at the top of the gunwale. If using a rowboat, you could offer to row the tender, but do not offer to do things you are not capable of performing.

Once you get on board, you may be asked to get the boat dry, which is called *pumping out the bilges*. Take off the sail covers and *gaskets* (sail ties), and once you are moving, take in the cushioning devices, or *fenders*, hung over the side. The usual procedure is to cast off, move out to sea under power, and set sail when already at sea.

If the boat is floating on a mooring, the rope or chain that secures the boat is part of the mooring and will be cast off and left behind. It will incorporate a float to be picked up with a boat hook on your return.

If the boat is anchored, you may be asked to help *weigh*, or pull up, anchor. The boat first moves ahead under power before the anchor is raised, and the chain is pulled in until it is vertical in the water. It is then relatively easy to break the anchor free from the bottom and winch it up. The anchor should normally be unshackled from the chain and then

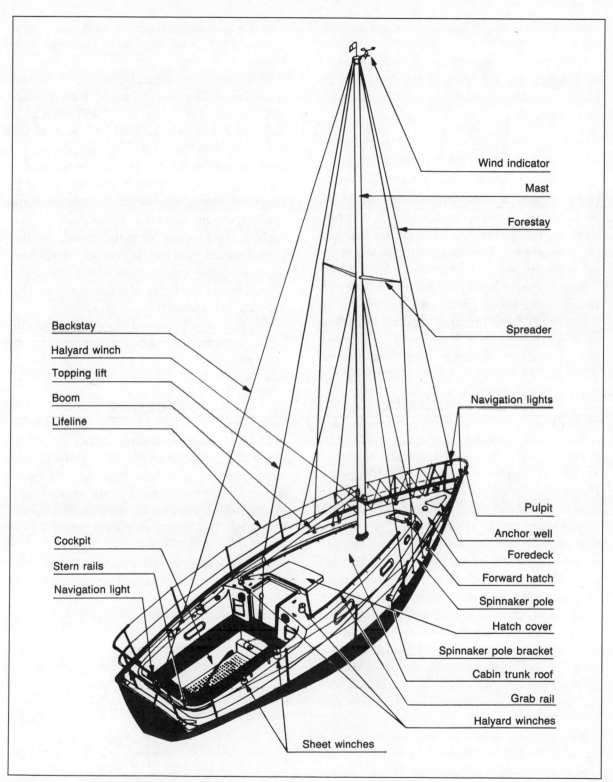

Figure 13-1 Parts of a typical cruiser

stowed below out of the way of the action on deck.

If the boat is at a marina, you may be asked to uncleat the mooring ropes that will be larger versions of what you have already encountered.

Hoisting Sails

You may be quite surprised at how similar the rigging is to what you're accustomed. As with hoisting sails on smaller boats, the halyard is attached to the head of the sail and then hauled up. The last few inches are hoisted with the aid of a winch.

The jibsheets need to be attached to the jib through the metal grommets, or *cringles*, in the corner of the jib, and bowline knots are ideal for this purpose. The sheets are then led aft, generally to a winch, and then cleated.

Trimming Sails

When the boat comes about, you may be asked to *skirt the jib*. This means that you should lift the foot of the jib in over the guardrails as it is being winched in tightly. A large boat comes about much slower than a dinghy. On the command "ready about," release the jibsheet all but the last two turns on the winch, and wait for the helmsperson to tell you to let go of the jibsheet. Some boats need to have the backwinding effect of the jib help them around. As soon as one jibsheet is let fly, the other is pulled in. At first, this is done hand over hand while there is no strain on the jibsheet. It must then be wrapped quickly around the winch and hauled tightly before the power of the wind in the jib makes this too difficult.

You may be asked to help set or lower a spinnaker. Listen carefully to what you are told to do because different crews use different techniques. If you are not clear about what you have been told to do, be sure to ask be-

fore the maneuver starts. A spinnaker boom is always set on the opposite side to the main boom.

Most bigger boats can be reefed. If the boat has roller reefing, the *topping lift* wire attached to the outer end of the boom will need to be tightened, the halyard will be lowered, and the boom will be rotated by a handle. The leech must be kept tight while the sail is rolled, and any battens in the way must be removed. Lastly, the halyard is tightened and the topping lift released. If the boat has jiffy reefing, the topping lift is tightened, the halyard lowered, and the luff cringle attached to a hook by the mast. Then the leech is tensioned before the halyard is tightened and the topping lift released.

You may also be asked to help change sails when the weather conditions alter or to gybe the spinnaker.

Steering

The boat may be steered either by a tiller or a wheel. Whichever you find, you will need to get the feel of it. You must know when a wheel is centered; usually one spoke end is decorated or marked in some way to show you when it is in the middle top (see Figure 13-2).

With a wheel when you want to turn to port, turn the wheel to port but be careful not

Figure 13-2 Wheel, showing center mark

to oversteer and move the tiller or wheel too much. Because a large boat responds to alterations more slowly, you may think you are getting no response, thus turning the helm even further. What is really needed is a little patience.

You may be asked to steer the boat on a compass course, or bearing. To do this accurately is a challenge. You will soon realize how the wind is changing in direction and speed and how this needs constant small adjustments from the helm.

Keep a good lookout all the time, but especially when you are steering, and report any boats to the skipper. In confined channels the rule is to keep to the right of oncoming boats.

Cleating and Winching

Because the weight of everything is much greater, make sure that the first thing you do when asked to cleat something is to get one complete turn around the cleat. This will hold quite heavy loads while the job is completed. When using winches, wrap all ropes around them clockwise. Be sure each turn goes neatly above the previous one for easy winching and freeing. Avoid making *riding turns*, which go on top of others, as they will jam (see Figure 13-3).

Winches are rotated when under strain by inserting a winch handle, which is taken out again when the rope has been cleated. Some

winches are two speed: Rotating one way gives one speed, and rotating the other way gives another speed. Dropping a winch handle overboard is a good way to ensure that you are not invited back again. Do be careful with them and stow them safely after use.

You may be asked to *tail a winch*, which involves taking up the slack in the rope. To do this, you need to keep the tension on the rope as it comes off the winch. You do not need to pull hard, but do not let the rope slip on the winch drum. Self-tailing winches (see Figure 13-4) do this job for you.

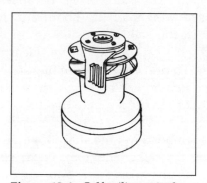

Figure 13-4 Self-tailing winch

Setting Up the Backstays

You may be asked to tension or release the backstays holding up the mast, which is called *setting up the backstays*. The windward one is under tension and the leeward one is let off to allow the boom to go over further. When coming about, the time to change them is when the boat is head to wind. Both can be on together, and the new windward backstay must be set before it takes the strain. When gybing, put the new one on as soon as the boom is clear of it, and then release the other. Be sure they are never both off together in a gybe, or you may be dismasted! Usually the helmsperson lets off the old backstay and the crew sets the new. Timing is critical in this maneuver, as in many others, so if you do not

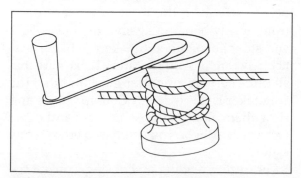

Figure 13-3 Riding turn on a winch

fully understand what your responsibility is, say so before the maneuver starts. No one minds explaining something again to eliminate any misunderstanding and thus prevent mistakes.

Rigging a Preventer

As you already know from your dinghy sailing experience, you must beware of an accidental gybe when sailing on a dead run. In a small boat, an accidental gybe may result in a capsize; in a large boat, because of the increased weight of the boom and greater power in the sail, the results of an uncontrolled gybe can be expensive. Gear can be broken. To prevent this from happening, rig a *preventer* on the boom. A preventer is a rope that fixes the boom to the leeward side. First, rig the preventer (where depends on the rig of each boat; ask the skipper where to rig it if you are doing this job). Next, ease the boom all the way out and tighten the preventer. Finally, haul the mainsheet in tightly, and secure the boom in position. You will become a valued crew member if you remember to alert the helmsperson that a preventer is rigged when everyone else has forgotten if you are on the point of gybing or coming about.

Returning to the Mooring, Anchorage, or Marina

When returning to a mooring marked by a float and you are asked to pick it up, use the boat hook to hook around the rope that leads down from the float. Do not try to hook the float itself. Immediately take a couple of turns around a cleat with the mooring rope/chain to hold the boat.

You may be asked to help anchor again at the end of the day. Get the anchor fixed back onto the end of the anchor chain and have it ready to let go at the bow. Lay out on deck the length of chain you expect to use and make it fast at that point. Head the boat slowly into the wind and stop. Just as she begins to slip backward, the crew drops the anchor. Wait until you see the tension go off the chain, indicating the anchor is on the bottom, then let out a few more feet, and fix the chain quickly on a cleat before there is tension on the chain. When the boat is stationary, more chain is let out to a ratio of at least 5:1 chain to water depth (see Figure 13-5).

Recleat the chain and check that the boat will not swing around to hit anything if the wind changes.

If you come alongside, be sure to put the fenders over the gunwale in good time. Three to a side is sufficient as long as you put them overboard at the widest part of the hull. Be ready to jump ashore with a line and fix it around a cleat when told to.

Making the Boat Shipshape

Stay on board long enough to help tidy up and leave the boat shipshape. Remember how tidy she was when you stepped aboard? You should leave her in at least as good or better shape. Help to furl the sails, put on the gaskets and sail covers, and remove halyards from along the mast; then attach them to a point away from the mast to prevent them from noisily banging against the mast. Fold and stow jib(s) and spinnaker(s), being particularly careful with the latter. Make sure that all three corners are uppermost and that the spinnaker is not twisted. Coil up sheets and stow them along with seat covers and other loose gear. Maybe you could also offer to row ashore.

For further reading on cruising, consult the Resources section.

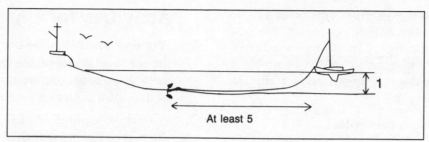

Figure 13-5   Anchor chain length

Checkpoints for Crewing on Larger Boats

1. If you are nervous about steering on a run, you could

   (a) ask that a preventer be rigged;

   (b) ask to sail on a broad reach course instead; or

   (c) watch the sail very carefully and at the first hint of a gybe, swing the wheel to windward.

2. If you have problems winching in a rope,

   (a) rehearse in your mind beforehand which way you will wrap the rope around the winch;

   (b) work quickly to get at least a couple of turns around it before there is any load; and

   (c) start cranking the winch handle as soon as the rope is difficult to pull in by hand.

Questions on Chapter 13

1. Name these parts of a cruiser:

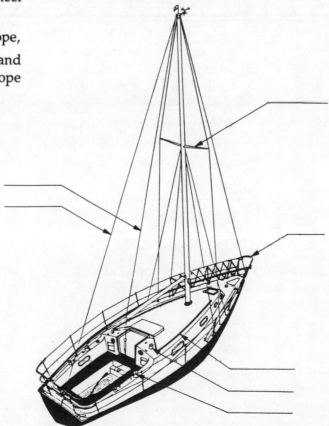

2. What two things must you be careful to avoid when winching a rope?

3. (a) What are the backstays?

   (b) What does it mean to set up the backstays?

4. (a) What is a preventer?

   (b) Why might one be rigged?

5. How much anchor chain should be used relative to the depth of the water?

Activities for Chapter 13

1. When you arrive at the boat, think about the various parts of the boat and their uses. If possible, arrange to arrive early so that the skipper can show you around.

2. With the cooperation of the skipper and the rest of the crew, ask if you can practice coming about and gybing maneuvers to become thoroughly acquainted with your assignment.

Test Yourself on Part 3

1. Which boat has the right-of-way in each racing situation and why? (2 points each; 10 points total)

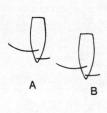

A   B

(a)

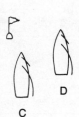

C   D

(b)

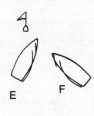

E   F

(c)

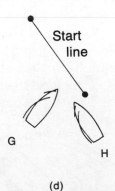

Start line

G   H

(d)

I   J

(e)

2. State two items you might consider when planning your start. (1 point each; 2 points total)

3. You are in second place, about three boat's lengths behind the leader. Give two possible tactics you could use to get ahead. (1 point each; 2 points total)

4. What is the most efficient course from A to B to C to A? (1 point each leg; 3 points total)

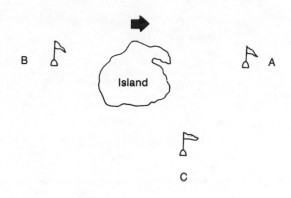

5. (a) What is a layline?

   (b) How can you judge it? (1 point each; 2 points total)

6. Explain the function of the following sailboard parts:

   (a) inhaul
   (b) uphaul
   (c) outhaul
   (d) downhaul (1 point each part; 4 points total)

7. (a) What takes the place of a rudder/tiller on a sailboard?

(b) How do you head up? (1 point each; 2 points total)

8. How do you know when a boat's wheel has the rudder centered? (1 point; 2 points total)

9. Explain the meaning of

   (a) gaskets
   (b) fenders
   (c) skirting the jib
   (d) tailing a winch
   (e) topping lift (1 point each; 5 points total)

Scores:

32-30 Excellent. You have a thorough knowledge of sailing.

29-25 Good. Just a few points to get clear.

24-20 Fair. Try rereading the chapters.

Below 20 Poor. Do not give up. First, reread the chapters, and then ask your more experienced friends or your instructor to clarify the points about which you are unclear. Next, repeat the Activities sections and then retake the test.

Try to get as much experience as possible on the water in all types of situations and keep an open mind, ready to learn new information about sailing.

You should be hooked by now! To increase your knowledge of a particular type of sailing, consult the Resources section, and then get out and test your new skills.

Good sailing!

Appendix A

Beaufort Scale

Beaufort force	Description	Knots	MPH	Land signs	Sea signs
0	Calm	<1	<1	Smoke rises vertically	Sea like a mirror
1	Light air	1-3	1-3	Smoke drifts	Ripples
2	Light breeze	4-6	4-7	Leaves rustle	Small wavelets
3	Gentle breeze	7-10	8-12	Twigs move; Light flags expended	Large wavelets, some breaking
4	Moderate breeze	11-16	13-18	Paper blows, small branches move	Frequent white-caps
5	Fresh breeze	17-21	19-24	Small trees sway	Many whitecaps; some spray
6	Strong breeze	22-27	25-31	Large branches move, telegraph wires whistle	Long waves, foam crests, and spray
7	Near gale	28-33	32-38	Whole trees move, hard to walk	Foam blown in streaks
8	Gale	34-40	39-46	Twigs broken off	Moderately high waves; crests blown off
9	Strong gale	41-47	47-54	Structural damage	High waves; spray mars visibility
10	Storm	48-55	55-63	Rarely inland; trees uprooted	White water everywhere
11	Violent storm	56-63	64-71	Extensive damage	Air filled with spray; huge waves
12	Hurricane	>63	>72	Total destruction	Totally confused sea

Appendix B

A Albacore	**↲** Banshee	**J** Bluejay	Comet	**DS** Day Sailer
El Toro	**E** Enterprise	Finn	Fireball	**F** Firefly
5O5 505	**FD** Flying Dutchman	Flying Fifteen	**FJ** Flying Junior	**14** 14
420 420	**470** 470	GP 14	**G** Graduate	Laser
L14 Lido 14	Lightning	Merlin Rocket	**MS** Minisall	**M** Mirror
N Naples Sabot	O.K. Dinghy	**Ω** Omega	**Q** Optimist	Peanut
Puffer	Snipe	Soling	**S** Sprog	**★** Star
Sunfish	Thistle	Topper	Tornado	**W** Wayfarer

127

Appendix C

Addresses of National Sailing Authorities

Australia

Australian Yachting Federation
33 Peel Street
Milson's Point
N.S.W., Australia 2061

Canada

Canadian Yachting Association
333 004 River Road, 11th Floor
Vanier
Ottawa, K1L 8B9
Ontario
Canada

New Zealand

New Zealand Yachting Federation
P.O. Box 4173
Auckland
New Zealand

United Kingdom

Royal Yachting Association
Victoria Way
Woking
Surrey GU21 1EQ
England

United States of America

United States Yacht Racing Union
Box 209
Newport, RI 02840
U.S.A.

Appendix D

Answers to Questions

Chapter 1

1. (a) vertical pole to which sails are attached

   (b) sailing in the same direction as the wind is blowing

   (c) direction from which the wind blows

   (d) sailing across the wind

   (e) floating part

   (f) configuration of sail(s) and mast(s)

   (g) movable fin down through boat to reduce side slip

   (h) heading into the wind; having a flapping sail

   (i) sailing at 45° to the wind; zigzagging upwind

2. because the sail flaps and produces no forward thrust

3. (a) reaching (b) running (c) beating

4.
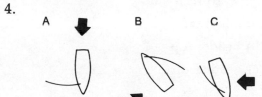

5.   A   B   C

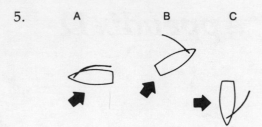

Chapter 2

1. (a) beat
   (b) run
   (c) close/fine reach
   (d) reach
   (e) luff
2. (a) starboard
   (b) port
   (c) port
   (d) starboard
   (e) neither; luffing
3. (a) starboard reach
   (b) port beat
   (c) port beat
   (d) port run
   (e) starboard reach
4. between half out and all out on the left/port side
5. (a) C
   (b) buoy is to leeward of A and to windward of B and C
6. (a) fallen off
   (b) headed up
   (c) headed up
   (d) fallen off
   (e) headed up

Chapter 3

1. turns her stern into the wind; turns away from the wind

2. to the sail side; to the leeward side; away from the helmsperson (if he/she is opposite sail)
3. (a) opposite from the sail; on the windward side
   (b) because you can balance the boat from this side
4. (a) across the boat
   (b) so that you can steer with the back hand and hold the sheet with the front hand
5. (a) about
   (b) gybed
   (c) gybed
6. (a) coming about is safer
   (b) because it happens slowly and without wind in the sail(s)
7. weather helm, which is corrected by "centering" the tiller slightly on the windward, or nonsail, side

Chapter 4

1. (a) fin at stern in water, which steers the boat
   (b) rope to control how far in or out boom/sail is
   (c) rope used to hoist sail
   (d) wire supporting mast
   (e) thin strip of wood/fiberglass inserted into sail to give it better shape
   (f) stick held by helmsperson and used for steering
2. (a) pulley
   (b) rope sewn into luff and/or foot
   (c) length of wood or metal at foot of sail
   (d) front of boat
   (e) fitting attaching boom to mast
   (f) left side looking forward

(g) right side looking forward

(h) track at stern over which sheet travels from side to side

(i) back of boat

3. (a) into the wind

(b) so that she does not "sail" as you rig her

4. (a) on the downwind, or leeward, side

(b) so that she will not be blown against the obstacle and damaged

Chapter 5

1. (a) rope at bow used for mooring or for being towed with

(b) boat tips over onto the sail side

(c) boat tips over onto the nonsail or helmsperson's side

(d) removing water from the boat

2. (a) life jacket/buoyancy aid to keep you afloat; sufficient clothing to keep you warm; nonslip shoes for traction and protection

(b) paddle/oars to give you alternative form of propulsion; bailer/scoop to bail the boat; painter for being towed with

3. hike out hard into the wind, opposite the sail; let the sheet out until the sail flaps; head the boat into the wind until the sail luffs

4. having too much weight on the windward side and then the wind dying suddenly

5. check everyone to ensure safety; check that all gear is secured so that it does not float away; head the boat into the wind to make righting easier; pull the centerboard all the way out to give a longer lever; lean on the centerboard to right the boat; get back in the boat to sail; remove water to make the boat more buoyant

6. check for breathing; turn victim over to drain out water; turn victim on side and strike back to dislodge debris; turn victim on back and pull jaw up; pinch nose and hold jaw; blow into victim's mouth until no longer necessary

7. divers in the vicinity

Part 1 Questions

1. (a) steering stick

(b) left side looking forward

(c) rope that controls how far in/out sail is

(d) metal/wood length at foot of mainsail

(e) rope used to hoist sail

(f) front of boat

(g) leading edge of sail

2. hike out to windward; ease the sheet out; head up into wind

3. d, c, a, g, b, e, f

4. any of the following: listen and feel for when your face is to the wind; flags, streamers, smoke, clouds, ripples, anchored boats, sails of boats

5. d, c, a, e, b

6. pull in the sheet until the sail stops flapping; fall off to go more with the wind until the sail is filled

7. let out the sheet and/or head into the wind; used for docking

8. you were not on a beat when you started to come about; use your paddle

9. start without delay

Chapter 6

1. anytime you feel uncomfortable about going out because of strong winds, offshore winds, lack of other boats, uncertainty about boat's ability to survive

2. (a) a beat

(b) so that you have only 90° to turn be-fore the wind will fill your sail(s) again

3. (a) to leeward

    (b) so that you cannot be blown against it

4. direction of the wind because you want to end up luffing; strength of wind, to judge when to head up; depth of water because you may have to remove the cen-terboard

5. any of the following: paddle/motor back, land elsewhere, and pull the boat back

Chapter 7

1. push the tiller briefly to the sail side; pull in the sheet

2. (a) watching the leading edge of the front sail

    (b) when it begins to luff, fall off a little; try to head up again without the sail luffing; when it does fall off; repeat.

3. (a) continually alter course slightly

    (b) because the wind changes

4. away from the sail to fall off a little

5. beating; sailing close-hauled

6. to be heading into the wind with the sails luffing; the boat will slow, stop, and make sternway

7. (a) an accidental gybe could occur

    (b) sail on a broad reach course instead

8. toward the sail side/to leeward/away from the helmsperson (when sitting opposite the sail)

Chapter 8

1. (a) pull the sheet half in

    (b) check it will be free to run out

2. by going the "long way" around and coming about

3. (a) the centerboard stops the boat making too much leeway

    (b) it is most needed on a beat/close-hauled course

    (c) it is least needed on a run

4. (a) half up

    (b) you are on a reach and making less leeway than when beating but more than when running

5.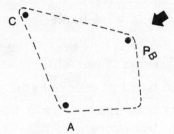

Chapter 9

1. wind strength, direction and steadiness; state of the water—size of waves; your own confidence; confidence in the boat; presence of others; weather forecast

2. (a) tipping the boat over onto the nonsail side, usually the side people are sit-ting on

    (b) caused by too much weight on that side for the wind, usually during a sudden drop in wind strength

    (c) avoid the situation by sitting in quickly

3. watch the surface of the water a few yards to windward; when you see dark wind-patches/catspaws, prepare for a gust

4. to reef is to reduce the size of the sail area being used; reef a boat by rolling the foot of the sail along the boom, or by tying reefing strings around the boom

5. (a) on the sail side

   (b) to help the sail take up a good airfoil shape

6. heavy weather—the boat is stopped by the waves;

   light weather—boat is only just moving and coming about may be enough to stop her altogether

7. shout "Man overboard" to draw everyone's attention to the fact; watch the victim constantly because once you lose sight of him or her, it may be difficult to find him or her again; reach away to give you time and space to maneuver; come about for safety; reach back because this is the reciprocal course; luff up to leeward of the victim so you do not sail over him or her and stop so you can haul the victim aboard

Chapter 10

1. (a) B on starboard

   (b) D on starboard

   (c) F to leeward

2. hull surface, electrolysis, sails, ropes, spars, rigging

3. advantages—strong, durable, ends easily sealed, may float

   disadvantages—causes rope burns, is hard on hands, is slippery, and nonflexible, and may float

4. (a) laid, braided

   (b) braided

   (c) kinder to hands, nonelastic, less likely to twist

5. standing part, bight

6. coil carefully, separate into 1/3 in throwing hand, throw underhand, retain hold of other end, throw over and beyond target

7. to join two ropes of different thicknesses

Part 2 Questions

1. (a) onshore

   (b) because you will be blown toward shore, not into open water

2. (a) reaching

   (b) because if you reach from A to B, you can also reach from B to A

3. any of the following: wind direction, wind strength, wind steadiness, currents, presence of other boats, weather forecast, your confidence in yourself, your confidence in the boat, whether someone else knows of your plans

4. (a) gybing accidentally

   (b) any of the following: be alert for reduced pressure on sail indicating gybe may be imminent; push the tiller immediately to the sail side; sail on broad reaches rather than runs

5. "ready about" when you have checked all around; "yes" or "OK," when crew is ready; "hard a-lee [lee-oh]," as you move the tiller across

6. marlinspike, pliers, knife

7. (a) U to leeward

   (b) X on starboard

   (c) Z to leeward; or Z being overtaken

8.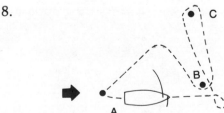

9. to port

Chapter 11

1. Alter course to reduce the danger of the impact. If you fail to take action to avoid a collision in which serious damage results, you may be held partly responsible, even though you held the right of way.

2. at the time of the preparatory signal, usually 5 minutes before the start

3. (a) B on starboard

   (b) D on starboard

   (c) F to leeward

   (d) H on starboard

   (e) J inside position, provided the overlap was established before two boat lengths of the mark

4. (a) protest

   (b) inform the other boat that you intend to protest, fly the protest flag, file a protest form on your return ashore

5. (a) X the windward end

   (b) you get a more favorable angle of approach to the course

6. (a) easier

   (b) let out the sail a little to go faster

7.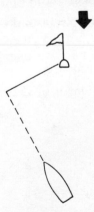

8.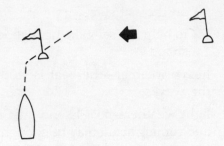

9. (a) duplicating what the boat behind you does to keep between your rival and the mark

   (b) when you are in the lead and only one boat is seriously challenging your position

   (c) if covertacking would put you in a less favorable position

Chapter 12

1. 1—boom, 2—outhaul, 3—downhaul, 4—shockcord, 5—uphaul, 6—inhaul

2. board perpendicular to the wind, sail upright and streaming away from wind, boom handle/end of uphaul in both hands

3. backward

4. raise the sail a little until the wind gets under it, use the wind to swing the sail across, and walk around the mast

5. rest sail on board and paddle; undo the clew outhaul; unstep the mast; fold boom up to mast; remove battens; place battens in mast sleeve; roll sail up in center of board; paddle

Chapter 13

1.
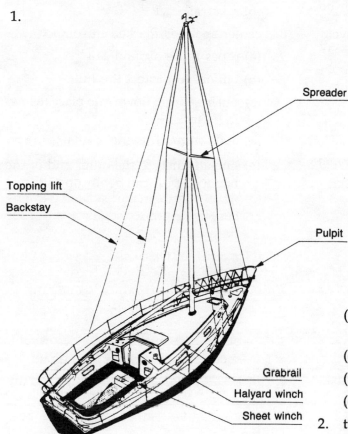

2. dropping the winch handle overboard; riding turns

3. (a) wire supports for the mast going from the masthead to the stern

   (b) to tension the new windward one and to release the new leeward one

4. (a) rope rigged to prevent movement, usually of a spar

   (b) on a dead run, rigged to prevent unexpected gybe

5. at least five times the depth

Part 3 Questions

1. (a) A, if she is being overtaken; B, if she is being overtaken; B, to windward

   (b) C, if she got her overlap in time; D if C did not get an overlap in time

   (c) F, on starboard

   (d) G, no room given at starting buoy

   (e) I, J is rerounding.

2. two from the following: time your approach from a fixed point; start at the favored end; start on starboard tack

3. Two from the following: get the other boat to covertack and bluff them into an unfavorable position; take a different course and hope you get better wind; concentrate hard on using all the windshifts

4.
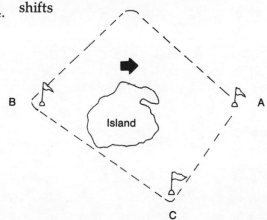

5. (a) the course to the windward mark from your present position with no further tacking

    (b) a course 90° from your present course, plus the effect of leeway

6. (a) to keep the boom tight against the mast

    (b) to pull the sail up with

    (c) to pull the sail tight along the boom

    (d) to pull the sail tight along the luff

7. (a) sail rake

    (b) rake sail back

8. center spoke is marked in some way

9. (a) ropes to tie around sail

    (b) buffers to protect the hull

    (c) pulling the jib down into place following a tack

    (d) gathering a rope off a winch

    (e) line attached to the outer end of the boom to pull the boom up with

Glossary

[Items in brackets are British terms]

Aback. A boat is taken aback when the wind strikes what had been the leeward side; the boat stops and may drift astern.

Abaft. Aft of the present position; toward the stern.

Abeam. Midway between dead ahead and dead astern; at 90° out to the side.

About. To come [go] about is to turn to the other tack by means of heading the bow into the wind; opposite is gybe.

Adrift. Loose and floating; no longer securely stowed.

Aft. At or toward the stern.

Ahead. In front of the boat.

Ahull. A boat lies ahull when she is purposely without sail or engine power and drifts beam on to sea and wind; used in heavy weather to ride out a storm.

Alee. Toward the leeward, or sheltered, side; "hard a-lee," said when tacking a boat, means the tiller has been put to the lee side.

All hands. The entire crew on board.

Aloft. Up above, in the mast, rigging, or sails.

Amidships. In the center of the boat.

Anchor. Device lowered overboard from the boat to the bottom, usually by means of chain, to secure the boat in position.

Anemometer. Device used to measure wind strength.

Apparent wind. Direction the wind appears to be blowing to those on board; a combination of the actual, or true, wind and the effect of the boat's movement.

Astern. Behind the boat; more toward the stern.

Backing a sail. Holding a sail to windward to catch the wind so the boat is slowed or made to tack.

Backing (wind). Counterclockwise shift in wind direction; opposite is veering.

Backstay. Wire running from masthead to deck at stern; may be one or two; if the latter, they may need setting and releasing when the boat tacks.

Backwind. One sail backwinds another when the airflow off the former goes onto the lee side of the latter.

Bail. To scoop out water.

Ballast. Extra weight, usually lead or water, in the hull for stability.

Bare poles. Sailing under bare poles is with no sails set; used in heavy weather to ride out a storm.

Batten. Narrow, flexible length of fiberglass or wood inserted into the leech of a sail to give better shape.

Batten pocket. Pocket in sail into which batten is inserted.

Beam. Width of the hull.

Beam reach. Direction of sailing exactly perpendicular to the wind.

Bear away/bear off. To change the boat's direction more away from the wind, or to leeward; opposite is to luff or head up.

Bearing. Direction of an object from the boat; compass course sailed.

Beating. Sailing close-hauled so as to make progress upwind.

Beaufort Scale. Scale of wind speed (see Appendix A).

Belay. To make fast or secure; to stop doing something.

Below. Downstairs or below deck.

Bend. To attach two ropes by means of a knot.

Bend on. To attach a sail to its spar.

Bight. Loop of a rope.

Bilge. Bottom part of boat where water may collect.

Bitter end. Last few inches of a chain or rope on board.

Blade. Main part of the rudder that projects into the water.

Blanketing. Blocking the wind from getting to another boat's sail; the leeward boat is said to be blanketed.

Block. Housing of wood or metal containing a pulley.

Boathook. Hook on the end of long pole designed for picking up moorings.

Bolt rope. Rope sewn into edge of sail.

Boom. Pole, or spar, along the foot of a sail.

Boomcrutch. Support on which the boom rests when the sail is lowered.

Bosun's chair. Seat used to haul someone up the mast.

[Bottlescrew]. See **Turnbuckle**.

Bow. Front of the boat; rhymes with cow.

Bowline (bō-lǐn). Knot making a loop that will not slip.

Bowsprit. Pole projecting forward from front of boat.

Braided rope. Rope made by braiding, or plaiting, strands instead of twisting them together.

Broach. When running, to accidentally turn parallel to waves and possibly be capsized.

Broad reach. Direction of sailing between beam reach and run.

Buoy. Marker that is floating and anchored.

Burgee. Racing flag, carried at head of sail.

By the lee. Sailing downwind when the boat would sail better with the sail on the other side; often precedes an accidental gybe.

Cam cleat. Cleat that holds a rope between two rotating sets of cam teeth, released by jerking rope perpendicular to the load.

Capsize. To tip the boat over on her side in the water.

Carvel. Wooden boat construction method where planks meet flush with each other.

Cast off. To let go the ropes securing the boat.

Catboat/rig. Rig with single, unstayed mast and no jib.

Catspaw. Isolated ruffling of water surface by wind.

Caulk. To seal gaps between planks.

Centerboard. Hinged fin protruding under boat, designed to minimize side slippage caused by wind.

Chain plate. Point of attachment of stays to hull, usually a thin metal strip.

Chandlery. Store selling marine equipment and supplies.

Chine. Line where sides and bottom of boat meet.

Chute. Either the spinnaker itself or a long sock into which a spinnaker is stowed for easy rehoisting.

Clam cleat. Cleat with grooved inner faces to grip rope.

Cleat. Device to which rope is made fast; to secure a rope.

Clew. Lower back corner of a sail.

Clinker. Wooden boat construction method where planks are laid so lower edge of one overlaps the plank below.

Clipper. Fast sailing ship of 19th century.

Close-hauled. Direction of sailing going as close to wind as possible without sail luffing; sail is hauled in close to hull.

Close reach. Direction of sailing between beam reach and beat.

Clove hitch. Knot used to tie around a spar.

Coaming. Ridge around the cockpit.

Cockpit. Sunken space within hull for crew.

Come about. See **About**.

Committee boat. Vessel from which sailing races are started.

Companionway. Ladder and passageway for going below deck.

Compass. Instrument indicating direction.

Covertacking. Tactic in racing to duplicate what an opponent astern does so as to keep between the opponent and the mark, or wind.

Cradle. Framework that supports a boat's hull when ashore.

Crew. All those aboard, excluding the helmsperson; or all on board.

Cringle. Metal ring in sail.

Cross trees. Spar on mast perpendicular to mast.

Cruiser. Boat with enclosed accommodation.

Cunningham hole. Cringle in tack for adjusting sail shape.

Cutter. Single-masted boat with more than one headsail.

Daggerboard. Movable fin protruding down through hull, like a centerboard, but unhinged.

Daysailer [Dayboat]. Small sailboat used for brief sails.

Deck. Floor of a boat.

Dinghy.   Small boat without fixed keel.

Dolly.   Wheeled frame used for moving and launching boats.

Douse.   To pull down.

Downhaul.   Rope used to pull something down.

Downwind.   Sailing more away from the wind than present position; downwind of is same as to leeward.

Draft [Draught].   Depth a boat needs to float.

Draw.   Sail that draws well is well trimmed or filled; a boat draws *x* feet where *x* is the draft.

Drop anchor.   To let go of the anchor to secure the boat in position.

Ease.   To reduce tension on or let out.

Ebb.   The outgoing or falling tide; opposite is flood.

Electrolysis.   A destructive chemical reaction between two metals in seawater; can be avoided by having like metals in contact.

Eye.   Permanent loop in rope or wire.

Fairlead.   Device used to guide a rope or wire.

Fall off.   To alter course to head more downwind; opposite is head up.

Fast.   To make secure.

Fathom.   Measure of depth equal to 6 feet or 1.83 meters.

Fend off.   To prevent from contacting another boat or dock.

Fender.   Device of plastic or similar used to protect hull from contacting another boat or dock; fenders hang over the gunwales and are pulled in when underway.

Fetch.   Length of fetch is the distance the wind blows over uninterruptedly; to fetch a mark is to reach it without further tacking.

Figure eight.   Stopper knot at end of sheet to stop rope running through pulley completely.

Fine reach.   Direction between beam reach and beat.

Flood.   The incoming or rising tide; opposite is ebb.

Fluke.   Protruding arm of anchor that lodges in sea floor.

Fly.   To fly a spinnaker is to set the sail; to let fly a rope is to let it go; the length of a flag from staff to end that flutters; the fluttering end is the fly.

Foot.   Bottom edge of sail.

Foresail.   Any sail set in front of the leading mast.

Forestay.   Wire holding up mast going from mast head to bow.

Forward.   Toward the bow, or front.

Foul.   Foul weather is heavy weather; a rope is fouled when tangled.

Freeboard.   Distance between top of gunwale and waterline.

Freshening.   Wind blowing more strongly.

Furl.   To take in and fasten a sail.

Gaff.   Spar on some rigs that supports the upper leading edge of sail.

Gale warning.   Weather forecast predicting winds of over 38 mph (33 knots).

Galley.   Boat's kitchen.

Gaskets.   Short lengths of rope used to secure a furled sail.

Genoa.   Large jib that overlaps the mainsail.

Gimbals.   Devices used to allow a table or stove to remain level while boat heels.

[Go about].   See **About**.

Gooseneck.   Point where mast and boom are joined; it is hinged and pivots.

[Goosewing]. See **Wing and wing.**

Grab rail. Length of wood or metal attached to cabin as a handhold.

Granny knot. Wrongly tied square knot with little strength.

Grommet. Eyelet in sail.

Ground tackle. Collective name for all anchoring and mooring equipment.

Guardrail. Fence along the edge of deck to prevent crew or gear from falling overboard.

Gudgeon. Ring part of rudder fitting into which pintle fits.

Gunter rig. Similar to gaff rigged, with a spar extending the mast up.

Gunwale. (gun 'l). Upper edge of boat's side.

Guy. Rope used to support or secure spar or sail; most commonly heard is the spinnaker guy, which is the windward sheet of the spinnaker.

Gybe. To change tacks by means of heading the stern into the wind; when running, a boat may gybe accidentally if the course is changed slightly or the wind direction changes so that the boat briefly runs by the lee; opposite is about.

"Gybe-oh." Command given when tiller is moved to make boat gybe.

Half hitch. Formed by crossing rope over standing part, then pulling it up through loop.

Halyard. Rope used to hoist or lower a sail.

"Hard a-lee." Command given when tiller is moved to make boat come about.

Harden up. See **Head up.**

Hawsepipe. Metal pipe down which anchor chain goes.

Head. Top corner of sail; boat's toilet.

Head to wind. Pointing into the wind so the sails luff.

Head up. To change a boat's direction to head more toward the wind; same as harden up; opposite is to fall off.

Header. Change in wind direction to more in front of boat; opposite is a lift.

Heading. Direction in which a boat is pointing.

Headsail. Sail set in front of the leading mast.

Headway. Forward progress through the water; opposite is sternway.

Heave. To pull on or throw a rope; a boat heaves when she moves up and down.

Heave to. To stop trying to make forward progress by setting sails to keep the boat on station.

Heel. To lean over; the lower end of the mast.

Helm. Steering devices, tiller or wheel, and rudder; see **Lee helm** and **Weather helm.**

Helmsperson. The person steering the boat.

Hiking stick. Extension to tiller; used when hiking out.

Hiking strap. Strap for feet, enabling crew to hike out.

Hull. Floating part of the boat.

In irons. When a boat tries to come about and fails, stopped halfway, luffing, she is in irons.

Inhaul. Rope that keeps boom tight against mast on sailboard.

Jam/jamb cleat. See **Cam cleat.**

Jaws. At lower end of gaff, the jaws encircle the mast.

Jib. Sail rigged in front of the leading mast.

Jibe. See **Gybe.**

Jibsheet. Rope used to control jib.

Jibsnaps [Jibhanks].   Devices used to attach jib to forestay.

Jury rig.   Any emergency rig using what remains after breakage.

Kedge.   Type of anchor; to pull a boat off from being aground by throwing out the anchor and hauling in on the anchor line repeatedly.

Keel.   Center of boat's bottom that runs fore and aft.

Ketch.   Two-masted rig where aft mast is smaller than main.

[Kicking strap].   See **Vang**.

Knot.   Configuration of rope; the speed of one nautical mph.

Lacing.   Tying of sails onto spars; twine wound between lifelines to stop sails blowing off deck.

Laid rope.   Rope twisted together, usually in three strands.

Land breeze.   Wind that blows from land to sea; same as offshore breeze; opposite is sea breeze.

Lash.   Make secure.

Lay up.   Rest boat from sailing, usually on cradles ashore.

Layline.   Course to next mark without further tacking.

Lee.   See **Leeward**.

Lee helm.   Tendency of the boat to head more downwind if the tiller is let go; opposite is weather helm.

Leech.   Back edge of sail.

["Lee-oh"].   See **"Hard a-lee."**

Leeward (loo′ard).   Side away from the wind, the more sheltered side; opposite is windward.

Leeway.   Sideways drift of a boat, caused by pressure from wind which the center- or daggerboard tries to counter.

Lift.   Change in wind direction to more astern; opposite is a header.

Line.   Strictly speaking, any rope aboard ship is a line.

Loose-footed.   Type of rig where the foot of the sail is attached to the boom only at the tack and clew.

Luff.   Leading edge of the sail; to luff is to point the bow into the wind so the sails flap; opposite is to bear away.

Luffing match.   Racing tactic where leeward boat tries to prevent windward boat from overtaking by luffing her, or forcing her head to wind.

Mainmast.   Principal mast.

Mainsail.   Principal sail on the mainmast.

Mainsheet.   Rope used to adjust mainsail.

Make fast.   To secure.

Mark.   See **Buoy**.

Marlinspike.   Thin, pointed metal tool used in rope work.

Mast.   Vertical pole from which sails hang.

"Mast abeam."   Racing term shouted by windward boat to curtail the luff of a leeward boat in a luffing match when the windward helmsperson is abeam of the leeward boat's mast.

Mast foot.   Bottom end of mast, same as mast heel.

Mast head.   Top end of mast.

Mizzen.   Aftermost sail of a three-masted boat.

Moor.   To secure boat at dock or on mooring.

Mooring.   Place where a boat makes fast.

Nautical mile. 6,076 feet or 1,852 meters; 1 nautical mph = 1 knot.

Navigation lights. Lights required by law to be shown aboard at night.

Neap tide. Small rise and fall of waterlevel; opposite is spring tide.

No-go zone. Sector in which a boat may not make forward progress; a boat luffs within the sector which is approximately 45° either side of the wind, for a total of 90°.

Oarlock. Device securing and giving leverage to an oar.

Offshore wind. Wind blowing from land to sea, also called a land breeze; opposite is onshore.

One design. Class of identical racing boats.

Onshore wind. Wind blowing from sea to land, also called a sea breeze; opposite is offshore.

Ooching. Illegal procedure of the crew lunging forward suddenly to impart forward momentum to the boat.

Outhaul. Rope used to pull something out away from the boat.

Overlap. During a race when neither boat is clear ahead or astern.

Overstand. To go on too far beyond the layline, thus wasting time.

Paddle. Small oar used without oarlock.

Painter. Rope attached to the bow for making fast or being towed with.

Partners. Small plates of wood or metal that frame the mast at deck level.

Peak. Upper back corner of a four-sided sail.

Pennant. Long, narrow triangular flag.

PFD. Personal Flotation Device, life jacket, or buoyancy aid.

Pile. Wooden or concrete post used for boats to moor onto.

[Piling]. See **Pile**.

Pinch. To sail too close to the wind so that the sail begins to luff and the boat slows down.

Pintle. Pin on the leading edge of the rudder and the stern, which slots into the gudgeon.

Pitchpole. Boat is thrown end over end by huge wave.

Planing. When the boat goes so fast the hull rises, friction is reduced, and speed increases rapidly.

Plot. A position on a chart; to plan a course.

Plug. Device in bottom of hull which is removed for draining.

Points of sailing. Headings of a boat relative to the wind direction such as run, reach, or beat.

Port. Left side when looking forward; port light is red; opposite is starboard.

Port tack. Boom is on the starboard side.

Preventer. Short length of rope to keep something in place, typically rigged to keep the boom from gybing on a run.

Protest flag. Signal, usually International Code Flag B, flown by boat to indicate she intends to file a protest as a result of some incident.

Pulpit. Rail around the front of the boat and the area it encloses.

Pumping. Frequent and rapid trimming of the sails designed to fan a boat around a course; illegal if done repeatedly for the purpose of propelling a boat in a race.

Purchase. Arrangement of ropes and pulleys to give mechanical advantage.

Quarter.   Direction out from the boat over the corner between side and stern.

Rake.   Angle a mast is tilted forward or back.

Ratlines (răt lĭns). Ropes crossing shrouds forming a ladder on old boats.

Reaching.   Course sailed at 90° to the wind.

"Ready about."   Command to crew to get ready to change tack by means of heading the bow into the wind.

Reef.   To reduce sail area in heavy weather so the boat may be more easily kept upright.

Reef cringles.   Metal rings around holes in sails through which ropes are passed to reef a sail.

Reef points.   Short lengths of twine attached to the lower parts of a sail that are taken around the boom and tied together under the boom in a reef or square knot to reef.

Ride.   To lie at anchor.

Riding lights.   Lights required to be displayed at night when a vessel is at anchor.

Riding turn.   Turn of a rope around a winch on top of a turn below; likely to jam.

Rig.   Configuration of masts and sails; to put up mast and standing rigging.

Rigging.   All nonstructural items aloft such as stays and sheets; see **Running rigging** and **Standing rigging.**

Roach.   The convex curve aft of the leech of a mainsail.

Roll tack.   Method of coming about quickly; usually used in light airs where crew roll boat across onto new tack.

Roller reefing.   Reducing sail area by rolling mainsail around boom, thus not needing reef points.

Rolling hitch.   Knot used to make fast a rope to a spar; better than clove hitch when strain will be parallel to spar.

[Rowlock].   See **Oarlock.**

Rubbing strake/strip.   Long, thin piece of wood or rubber running along length of gunwale to protect boat.

Rudder.   Vertical fin in water at stern by which boat is steered.

Running.   Direction of sailing with the wind.

Running lights.   See **Navigation lights.**

Running rigging.   Rigging that moves, such as halyards.

Sailing by the luff.   Using the fluttering luff of the sail to tell you when you are sailing too close to the wind for your sail setting.

Sailing to leeward.   Sailing away from the wind as in running.

Sailing to windward.   Sailing toward the wind as in beating.

Schooner.   Boat with two or more masts, the foremast being shorter than the mainmast.

Scull.   To use an oar over the stern; to propel the boat by moving the tiller rapidly back and forth.

Sea anchor.   Floating or submerged item used to keep the bow into the wind and sea.

Sea breeze.   Wind blowing from sea to land; opposite is land breeze.

Set.   To set a sail is to hoist and use it.

Shackle.   Small D-shaped fitting with a removable pin.

Shake.   To shake a reef is to remove it and sail with full sail.

Sheave.   Rotating wheel inside a pulley over which rope passes.

Sheet.   Rope that controls how far in or out a sail is.

Ship.   Either to bring on board or to fix in place for sailing.

Shrouds.   Wire supports for mast, running from masthead to gunwales.

Skeg.   Small fin under center of hull at stern.

Skirt. To skirt the jib is to pull the foot into place following a tack or gybe; in large boats the jib may be caught on the rails.

Slack tide/water. Time when the tide is changing and hence hardly moving.

Sleeve. Some sails are rigged to the mast by fitting over it like a sleeve.

Sloop. Single-masted boat with one jib.

Small craft advisory. U.S. National Weather Service warning of forecast of winds 18 knots or higher.

Sounding. To take a sounding is to measure depth.

Spar. Long, thin pole such as mast, boom, or gaff.

Spill. To spill wind is to allow wind to escape from the sail so that less power drives the boat.

Spinnaker. Large sail, often brightly colored, set at bow when sailing on run or reach.

Spinnaker pole. Spar used to hold windward clew of spinnaker.

Splicing. Joining of two ends of rope by weaving together.

Spreaders. Like crosstrees, designed to spread load from shrouds.

Spring. Mooring rope rigged at angle to boat.

Spring tide. High and low water occurring twice per month at new and full moon; opposite is neap tide.

Sprit. Small spar used for extension of sail away from boat.

Squall. Sudden strong wind, usually of short duration.

Squarerigged. Sails are all rectangular.

Squaresail. Rectangular-shaped sail.

"Stand by to gybe." Command given to prepare crew for gybe.

Standing part of rope. The long part away from the part being knotted.

Standing rigging. Rigging that is fixed, such as the shrouds.

Starboard. Right side when looking forward; starboard light is green; opposite is port.

Starboard tack. Boom is on the port side.

Stays. Wires supporting mast fore and aft; to be in stays is to be luffing.

Staysail. Sail set on stay between masts.

Steerage way. Sufficient forward movement for rudder to turn boat.

Stem. Upright post at bow.

Step. Socket into which foot of masts fits; to step a mast is to raise it into place.

Stern. Back end of boat.

Sternway. Backward progress through the water; opposite is headway.

Stock. Cross piece of anchor; vertical shaft of rudder.

Stow. To put away.

Sweat up. To hoist tightly.

Tack. Lower front corner of sail; heading of boat in relation to wind (e.g., on port tack); to tack is to come about.

Tacking. Sailing a zigzag course against the wind.

Tail a winch. To put turns around and guide them off the winch.

Telltales. Small lengths of wool or nylon attached to a sail so that they flutter just before the sail would luff.

Tender. Small boat carried on board a larger one, often used to ferry crew ashore.

Thimble. Egg-shaped fitting, often of plastic, in eye of rope to protect from wear.

Throat. Upper front corner of a four-sided sail.

Thwart.   Any seat going across the hull.

Tide.   Rise and fall of sea level caused by effect of moon and sun.

Tiller.   Stick used to steer boat.

[Tiller extension].   See **Hiking stick.**

[Toe strap].   See **Hiking strap.**

Topping lift.   Rope attached to outer end of boom used to raise boom to take weight off it.

Track.   Groove in mast or boom into which sail is slid.

Transom.   Flat, after end of boat.

Trapeze.   Wire from mast to which crew is attached to hike out when standing on gunwale.

Traveller.   Device enabling block, typically on mainsheet, to move across boat.

Trim.   Difference in draft between bow and stern; to trim sail is to adjust its angle to the wind.

[Trolley].   See **Dolly.**

True wind.   Actual direction the wind blows as distinct from apparent wind.

Turn.   To take a turn around a cleat is to wind a rope around.

Turnbuckle.   Tensile attachment of shrouds to gunwale.

[Una rig].   See **Catboat.**

Uphaul.   Rope on sailboard used to haul sail upward.

Upwind.   Closer to wind, to windward.

Vang.   Line attached to spar, typically the boom, to hold it in place.

Veering (wind).   Clockwise shift in wind direction; opposite is backing.

"Water."   Called for by racing boat when she deems she needs room to maneuver.

Way.   Movement through the water.

Weather.   Same as windward; to weather a storm is to survive it.

Weather helm.   Tendency of a boat to head up; opposite is lee helm.

Weather mark.   Buoy of course reached by beating to it.

Weigh anchor.   To raise the anchor.

Whip.   To prevent the end of a rope from unravelling by wrapping twine tightly around it.

Whisker pole.   Small spar used to boom out jib when running.

Whitecaps [Whitehorses].   White, broken water on wave.

Winch.   Drum with mechanical advantage used for winding in rope.

Windshadow.   Area with little or no wind sheltered by a boat or other structure.

Windshift.   Change in wind direction; see **Backing** and **Veering, Header** and **Lift.**

Windward.   Side the wind blows over first; opposite is leeward.

Wind direction.   Direction from which wind blows.

Wing and wing.   Running with main and jib on opposite sides.

Wishbone.   Type of boom of wishbone shape on either side of sail as on a sailboard.

Yard.   Large spar from which sails are hung.

Yawl.   Rig with two masts where the smaller, aft mast is aft of the rudder.

Resources

Bond, B. (1980). *The handbook of sailing.* New York: Alfred A. Knopf.

Creagh-Osborne, R. (1977). *This is racing.* Boston: Sail Books.

Denk, R., & Kimball, A. (1980). *The complete sailing handbook.* New York: Mayflower.

Elvstrom, P. (1985). *Paul Elvstrom explains the yacht racing rules: 1985 rules.* London: Adlard Coles.

Hiscock, E.C. (1981). *Cruising under sail.* London: Oxford University Press.

New Glenans sailing manual, The (1978). Boston: Sail Books.

Pinaud, Y.-L. (1980). *Sailing: From start to finish.* London: Adlard Coles.

Royce, P.M. (1982). *Sailing illustrated.* Ventura, CA: Western Marine Enterprises.

Sleightholme, J.D. (1982). *This is sailboat cruising.* New York: State Mutual Book.

Twiname, E. (1983). *Start to win* (2nd ed.). London: Adlard Coles.

Winkler, R., & Stanciu, U. (1979). *This is windsurfing.* Boston: Sail Books.

Winner, K., & Jones, R. (1980). *Windsurfing with Ken Winner.* San Francisco: Harper and Row.

Index

About the Author

Author Shirley Reekie has been an avid sailor since she first learned to sail with her father at four years of age in her native Great Britain. She is certified as an instructor by the Royal Yachting Association and is a member of the U.S. Yacht Racing Union. Shirley has competed at the regional and national levels and has served as fleet captain for a competitive sailing club in the United Kingdom. She is presently the faculty advisor to the San Jose State University sailing club and racing team. Shirley received her bachelor degree from the University of Liverpool, and masters degree from the University of Leeds before completing her PhD in physical education from The Ohio State University. Currently, she serves as lecturer at San Jose State University teaching international and comparative sport, history, research methods, and sailing. In addition to sailing, Shirley relaxes by playing the bagpipes.